Mapping the Big Picture

Integrating Curriculum & Assessment K–12

Heidi Hayes Jacobs

ASCD

Association for Supervision and Curriculum Development
Alexandria, Virginia USA

Association for Supervision and Curriculum Development
1703 N. Beauregard St. • Alexandria, VA 22311-1714 USA
Telephone: 1-800-933-2723 or 703-578-9600 • Fax: 703-575-5400
Web site: http://www.ascd.org • E-mail: member@ascd.org

Gene R. Carter, *Executive Director*
Michelle Terry, *Assistant Executive Director, Program Development*
Nancy Modrak, *Director, Publishing*
John O'Neil, *Acquisitions Editor*
Julie Houtz, *Managing Editor of Books*
René Bahrenfuss, *Copyeditor*
Deborah Whitley, *Proofreader*
Gary Bloom, Director, *Design and Production Services*
Karen Monaco, *Senior Designer*
Tracey A. Smith, *Production Manager*
Dina Murray, *Production Coordinator*
Valerie Sprague, *Desktop Publisher*

Printed in the United States of America.

May 1997 member book (p). ASCD Premium, Comprehensive, and Regular members periodically receive ASCD books as part of their membership benefits. No. FY97-7.

ASCD Stock No.: 197135   ASCD member price: $13.95   nonmember price: $16.95

Library of Congress Cataloging-in-Publication Data

Jacobs, Heidi Hayes.
      Mapping the big picture : integrating
curriculum and assessment K-12 / Heidi Hayes
Jacobs.
            p.   cm.
      Includes bibliographical references (p.).
      ISBN 0-87120-286-7
      1. Teacher participation in curriculum
planning—United States. 2. Educational tests and
measurements—United States. I. Title.
LB2806.15.J33   1997
375'.001—DC21   97-16708
                                          CIP

03   02   7   6   5

In memory of A. Harry Passow—

a vigilante for common sense in the curriculum.

Mapping the Big Picture: Integrating Curriculum and Assessment K-12

About the Author

Heidi Hayes Jacobs has served as an educational consultant to numerous schools and educational organizations nationally and internationally. She has been an adjunct associate professor of the Department of Curriculum and Teaching at Teachers College, Columbia University, since 1981. Her book *Interdisciplinary Curriculum: Design and Implementation* has been a bestseller for ASCD. Her work is featured in various video series and numerous professional journals. Her doctoral work was completed at Columbia University's Teachers College in 1981. She lives with her husband and two children in Westchester County, New York. You may reach her at the phone number and e-mail address below.

Curriculum Designers, Inc.

914-921-2046

e-mail: curricdes@aol.com

1

The Need for Calendar-Based Curriculum Mapping

In the fall of 1988, I was asked to work with a New Jersey school district to help refine their curriculum articulation and integration. In a conversation with a 7th grade team, I asked, "What will you actually be teaching this year?" The English teacher smiled and responded, "You mean what will each of us actually be doing tomorrow?" I thought for a moment and answered, "Well, at least let's get an idea about September, October, and so on. How can we integrate the curriculum if we don't know what it is?"

At this point the building principal interjected, "But we do have our district curriculum guides." The science teacher looked skeptical: "Yes, but those aren't necessarily accurate. They are guidelines, but they are not exactly what we work on in class."

We began to lay out the year's plan on index cards across a library table, and one truth became evident. The one thing that the English, social studies, science, math, foreign language, technology, and art teachers had in common was September, October, and November. Each had to deal with the Gregorian calendar. And it became plain to me that by using the school calendar, the teachers could begin to create a realistic picture of their program in a clear, practical fashion.

Teachers always have used the school year calendar to make their plans. But in the past they have not had the technology to collect real-time information about the actual curriculum including content, skills, and assessment data. After my New Jersey experience, I began asking teaching teams at the elementary, middle, and high school level to try using the school calendar to collect basic information about their curriculum plans such as unit titles, projects, and materials. The response was consistently positive. Not only did people find the calendar an honest vehicle for communication about the curriculum, but they reported it was far more efficient than reading through lists of curriculum guidelines from other departments.

In October 1991, I wrote a short article for *Educational Leadership* on calendar-based mapping and received a strong response from around the country asking how to commence work on maps (Jacobs 1991). In the ASCD video *Integrated Curriculum* (1993), one of the segments shows a group of teachers creating curriculum maps. This sparked even more phone calls and faxes about how to do "this mapping thing." I decided that the concept needed more field research and scrutiny.

In the past few years, I have spent many hours with faculties around the country compiling the suggestions and successes summarized in this book. I have communicated with leading educators such as Mike Eisenberg (see Eisenberg and Johnson 1996), who demonstrates the value of using maps to inject information processing skills into the core curriculum, and Bena Kallick (see Costa and Kallick 1995), who solidly supports the notion of the "critical friend" and views mapping as a staff development opportunity for quality communication about curricular renewal.

It is now completely clear that educators can construct useful maps in just a few hours each school year, and these maps can change as often as needed to revise or reorder the curriculum. This book explains how to begin that task.

Why Map at All?

Though teachers may work together in the same building for years, they usually have sketchy knowledge about what goes on in each other's classrooms. High school teachers on the same corridor have no clue as to their colleagues' books, concepts, and assignments. A middle school team may work diligently on its specific program but have limited information about any other team in the building. Elementary schools can be nurturing environments but fundamentally a collection of one-room schoolhouses.

If there are gaps among teachers within buildings, there are virtual Grand Canyons among buildings in a district. It is rare to find a high school teacher who is knowledgeable about the middle school curriculum or elementary and middle school teachers who are in close communication about their students. The reality is an occasional "transition" meeting between feeding and receiving schools where cursory information is passed on, though with the best of intentions. All too often, curriculum decisions are made in a vacuum.

With so little real-time data available, we find two polarized tendencies. One is to become rigid and lock step with curriculum guides, giving the impression that all is under control. The second is to become so loose and vague that no one seems to have a clue as to what is going on.

To make sense of our students' experiences over time, we need two lenses: a zoom lens into this year's curriculum for a particular grade and a wide-angle lens to see the K–12 perspective. The classroom (or micro) level is dependent on the site and district level (a macro view).

Though the micro and macro levels are connected throughout a district, there is a conspicuous lack of macro-level data for decision making. Yet we need that big picture for each student's journey through his or her years of learning. With data from curriculum mapping, a school and its feeding and receiving sites can review and revise the curriculum within a larger, much-needed context. Data on the curriculum map can be examined both horizontally through the course of any one academic year and vertically over the student's K–12 experience.

In the past we relied on curriculum committees to provide the larger perspective. It is my contention that old-styled curriculum committees should be dismantled and replaced. Site-based curriculum councils creating curriculum maps with computers should focus on the most basic level of the students' experience in the individual school. District curriculum cabinets representing all the schools should meet periodically, taking on the role of a coordinating body akin to the editor-in-chief of a publishing house. These ideas are developed in Chapter 6 with details of specific roles and responsibilities.

We need to change the process used in making curriculum decisions because most curriculum committees are ineffective at actually producing work that directly affects student performance. Curriculum committees usually come together to formulate lists of objectives, skills, and concepts that are optimum goals for teachers to implement. Occasionally these lists inspire and focus teachers' actions, but too often they remain nothing more than lifeless inventories of isolated skills. The lists may discuss 1st grade writing skills or 3rd grade reading skills, but they offer little or no focus on precisely when specific skills will be addressed during the course of a school year, let alone a group of school years.

Without a commitment to *when* a skill will be taught, there is no commitment. Furthermore, skills are not taught in a vacuum. They are addressed in application to content, and they are evidenced in a product or performance by the learner. In short, though committees anguish over the skill list, most end up with the feeling that it is not a useful document. As one teacher put it, "There is a sense of let's get through this, because they're making us." District-level educators become all the more frustrated when the skill list is filed away, and no one really knows if and how the skills are used.

No teacher or administrator is to blame for this situation. None of us chooses to make the absence of efficient or effective communication a reality. It has long been difficult to find out or plan curriculum within a broader context. Teachers cannot run up and down the halls of their buildings with notepads gathering information about curriculum and assessment. They cannot call every teacher each student has had for the past few years. Constant meetings outside school hours are ineffective and expensive. We need a 21st century approach. Curriculum mapping amplifies the possibilities for long-range planning, short-term preparation, and clear communication.

Our students need us to know their experiences over the course of time. They need us to know what's really going on in their daily classes as they move among teachers and subjects. They need us to know and give credence to their work from year to year. With that information, possibilities emerge. The next chapter describes the procedures for compiling maps.

✧   ✧   ✧

2

Procedures for Curriculum Mapping

After years of working with many different faculties, I have developed a recommended sequence for creating and working with curriculum maps based on the school calendar. This chapter describes these tasks in seven phases. Certainly each school or district is unique, and each faculty has its own dynamic. A variable as basic as size of the faculty can make a huge difference in how something is accomplished. But these tasks are flexible and can be adapted to local conditions.

There are some important distinctions to be made between early work that pioneered mapping and contemporary possibilities. Before personal computers, mapping in the '70s and early '80s was influenced largely by Fenwick English, a prominent curriculum leader and powerful theoretician. In those days, mapping was accomplished through surveys and interviews conducted by an evaluator or coordinator. Teachers reported how much time they spent on topics to promote "alignment" (English 1980). As English stated, "Mapping is a technique for recording time on task data and then analyzing this data to determine the 'fit' to the officially adopted curriculum and the assessment/testing program" (1983 p. 13).

Because someone else met with teachers, recorded what they said, and typed up the findings, almost all maps went through a third party. Often there was a delay in typing and retyping findings. With computers, it is now possible to register more complete information about content, skills, and performance assessment in real time. More significantly, the task now is to show student work as it actually happens in the classroom *and* in relation to state or district standards.

The curriculum should grow and evolve in a dynamic fashion. I believe strongly that the integrity of the process rests on the individual teacher completing a map rather than going through another party. In the past, it was inefficient to do so. Now it is possible for teachers to easily complete maps, compile them, share them with colleagues, and communicate with educators in other buildings.

Phase 1: Collecting the Data

In this phase, each teacher describes three major elements that comprise the curriculum on the curriculum map:

• The processes and skills emphasized;

• The content in terms of essential concepts and topics, or the content as examined in essential questions (see Chapter 4); and

• The products and performances that are the assessments of learning.

Highly specific information about daily lesson plans isn't needed. The purpose of this phase is for each teacher to place realistic data about what he or she teaches in the course of the academic year on a macro level. I have found it of great help to show teachers a number of sample maps to model the level and type of work that is required (see Appendix III). Without sample maps, this description of mapping appears daunting. It is actually a very doable task. Perusing the maps in the Appendix might clarify the required degree of detail.

It is critical that each teacher completes a calendar-based map. No one can complete a map for anyone else; otherwise, the data are false. The only professional person who knows what is taught in the classroom is the teacher. Coordinators cannot fill out maps; principals cannot; department chairs cannot fill them out for everyone for the simple reason that they are not in each classroom. The purpose is to collect authentic data about the classroom and genuine information about what students actually experience—not what others think they are supposed to be studying. Whether the information is written on a large sheet of butcher paper with the months as headings, index cards, standard $8\frac{1}{2}$" by 11" sheets of paper, or the screen on a computer terminal, an extraordinary act occurs. Teachers using calendar-based maps share realistic data about the curriculum in their building.

A number of issues are commonly raised in this initial task. Some ask, "What if I don't teach in the disciplines? What if I teach themes?" The purpose of the map is to reveal what *is* actually going on in the curriculum, so the design of the map should reflect such themes.

Some teachers ask, "What if I only follow the students' interests, because we are an inquiry-based program?" In this instance, a more diary-based collection should occur, where teachers record the ongoing program in real-time. I have worked in a few schools reflecting this philosophy and find that they rely heavily on the maps to foster communication. Otherwise, no one knows from year to year what any given student has experienced.

Other teachers ask, "What if I don't teach to the months?" This question suggests a misunderstanding of the maps. The point is not to teach to the months but to use the months as a common reference to plot the classroom curriculum.

Another important tip is to give an approximate time frame for completing maps. Most schools attempt to cast a realistic draft of the year and amend the maps as they go. Others follow a "diary" method as previously mentioned, which requires a disciplined schedule. Most individual elementary teachers find it takes about one hour to complete the "content" portion of the map for one school year. Most secondary teachers find it takes about 45 minutes per course per year for content data alone. If teachers take significantly longer than this, there is some misunderstanding about the scope of the task or they do not want to complete the task.

The more demanding task is the completion of the skills and assessment components of the curriculum. This generally requires some serious reflection on the primary skills and the most important assessments that were targeted through the year. In a sense, it is a discrimination task. The map maker is selecting the most significant skill work and the most revealing assessments. But, even here, the time should not be overwhelming. It should take no more than twice the time to collect the content strand of the maps.

When the concept of mapping is presented to the faculty, a range of formats should be introduced. Select one consistent format for all to use. This makes data collection efficient. It is very important that teachers are comfortable with the format of the maps to ensure efficient data collection. Principals are wise to reassure teachers that mapping is not used for evaluation purposes. On occasion, I have seen reluctant staff members afraid that a principal is out to get them because they didn't get to the unit on "Preventing the Overuse of the Gerund in English" or the project on "My Trip to the Fire Department." Clarify the task of mapping and acknowledge that no one ever "does it all" during the course of the school year.

I suggest that faculty meeting time be provided for teachers to work on maps privately in their classrooms. Whether these first maps are done with paper and pencil or on a computer, eventually all maps will be on a computer. Any paper-and-pencil map can be entered in the computer by an aide or secretary if the teacher is unable to work with a computer. Clearly, the most striking and effective way to gather mapping data is on a computer. Push, nudge, and bargain for school leaders—both administrative and teacher—to use computers themselves. This is a way to take full advantage of not only immediate data gathering but networking and communication among buildings as well.

Phase 2: The First Read-Through

Once the maps are completed, each teacher becomes an editor for the map for the entire building. First, each faculty member should become familiar with his or her colleagues' curriculums as well as the scope of all the maps. Then, the teacher can carry out the "editing" tasks described in Chapter 3.

First, the teacher-as-editor reads through the maps to gain information. I recommend that teachers underline those content, skill, or assessment areas that are new to them. I frequently hear faculty members say, "I didn't know you taught that!"

The other tasks require a discerning eye. Teachers should look for repetitions, gaps, meaningful assessments, matches with standards, potential areas for integration, and timeliness (tasks described in greater detail in Chapter 3). When the teacher spots an area needing work, he or she should circle the area in need of revision. The teacher's task isn't to rewrite or even to make suggestions. Those judgements should be delayed. Instead, the job is to highlight areas for future examination.

Editors are caring but detached. They examine a manuscript for problems, but they do so in the context of improving quality. Because the influence of the curriculum is so tremendous on children and adolescents, they deserve no less than our most scrupulous, critical evaluation. When each teacher becomes a curriculum editor, the professional level of the entire school is elevated.

It is very important that teachers work alone for the first read-through. If a group of teachers starts out together, they may try to avoid offending someone, thus overlooking crucial problems in the map. But with a thorough, critical reading of the maps, each teacher gains an appreciation for his or her role in the flow of curriculum through the years, significantly more detailed knowledge of the school's curriculum, and insight into the school's needs. Then it is time to work collectively and meet in small groups to share observations.

The time frame for the individual teacher's read-through obviously depends on the number of classroom teachers in the building. A reasonable approximation for elementary schools is two to four hours; two to five hours is appropriate for middle schools and high schools. On the secondary level, some teachers deal initially with interdisciplinary teams and others deal with departments. The key is to follow the actual instructional pattern for learners in the building. Most schools use time already designated for department, area, or faculty meetings to do this work.

Phase 3: Mixed Group Review Session

When it's time for small group review, the groups should be composed of people who do not work together. Teachers should not work with their usual instructional grade-level team, interdisciplinary team, department, or teaching partner. Optimum size of the groups is six to eight staff members. The opportunity to share with familiar teacher teams and partners will come, but delaying that step only heightens the power of this process. When familiar groups review the maps, they tend unconsciously or consciously to homogenize the material so that it looks uniform. The result is an inaccurate portrayal of the school year.

In the mixed group review, each teacher shares his or her findings from the individual review of the maps. This is a reporting out procedure. It is not a decision-making procedure, and delaying judgment is critical. Hence, teachers should simply state the areas in which they gained information, the places where they located gaps, repetitions, potential areas for integration, mismatches between outcomes and curriculum, and meaningful and nonmeaningful assessments. They are "red-flagging" areas that need attention—not rewriting the curriculum.

It is helpful in this session for a facilitator to collect and report the findings of each member. A sheet listing the findings is an important outcome of the mixed group review. This sheet will assist the faculty in compiling the data for the next phase: the large group review of findings.

Phase 4: Large Group Review

All members of the faculty attend the large group review. Before this meeting, the facilitators of each small group review session have reported on the findings of the small group sessions. These findings are gathered in a chart encompassing all of the reporting sessions. The leader of the large group review, whether it is the principal or a teacher leader, posts these findings, then asks the audience to comment on emerging patterns. Both general and specific comments will arise. The key is to delay judgement again and simply compile data using each of the editing tasks that are outlined in Chapter 3.

Once overall findings are available to the large group, the faculty should examine the list carefully and take on the next two procedures. A critical decision at this juncture is whether to break into instructional units or stay as the larger group. A key variable is the size of the faculty. If you are in a small school where faculty size is 10 to 25, it is perfectly workable to stay in the large group. If the faculty is larger, then returning to instructional units—such as grade-level teams, house teams, or departments—makes greater sense. The important point here is that the faculty is now moving from a review mode to an editing, revising, and developing mode.

Phase 5: Determine Those Points That Can Be Revised Immediately

With lists of observations in hand, the faculty starts to sift through the data and determine areas that can be handled by faculty members, teams, and administrators. Frequently, there are glaring repetitions that can be addressed by the exchange of ideas between a few faculty members.

For example, in one elementary school both a 3rd and 4th grade team dealt with the Colonial Period in U.S. history. When students began to study the period again in 4th grade, they complained that they "had Colonial before." Given the packed nature of the 4th grade curriculum, the two grade-level teams negotiated and agreed that the 3rd grade would take over Colonial America and broaden the local and state perspective to include the other colonies. The 4th grade would move directly into the American Revolution, making more time to deal with areas where students had limited exposure, such as the Declaration of Independence. This maneuver did not require a school board meeting or a large curriculum committee report. It was a relatively straightforward negotiation.

I do not want to suggest that such points are always easily resolved. I recall a scene when a teacher stomped a foot down, refusing to rethink the placement of a 19th century British Authors unit: "No! I won't give up Dickens! Dickens is mine!" But it usually is much easier to handle problems if everyone sees the difficulty. The mapping process readily shows the repercussions of even a modest decision about the curriculum.

Phase 6: Determine Those Points That Will Require Long-Term Research and Development

While reviewing the maps, groups will find areas that require more in-depth investigation before a solution can be produced. This is obvious because the problem encompasses a range of grade levels or departments, the implications likely will include structural decisions, or the results of altering the curriculum will have long-term consequences.

For example, there might be a "gap" in a series of assessments between the elementary and middle school writing program. In this case teachers in both buildings need to examine a developmental sequence of writing over the course of time. The maps reveal that creative writing projects abound at both levels, but the only nonfiction writing listed at both levels is "reports." When will formal essay writing be introduced? When should note cards be introduced? Should 8th graders write position papers rather than simply reports as they did in 4th grade? The maps will give the elementary and middle school teachers an opportunity to settle these issues without blaming each other for the gaps. My experience is that mapping provides an opportunity for professional discussion about curriculum articulation and planning.

If a high school considers the possibility of interdisciplinary work for 9th graders, everyone will need time to examine the implications for school structures. The schedule and team configurations loom large in such undertakings. Before a decision is made, research about internal needs and external practices in other high schools is critical. Again, time is essential. Schools have used faculty meetings, release time, summer workshops, and other methods to provide the opportunity to study large and complex issues.

Perhaps a group of staff members reviews the K–12 maps and sees the absence of district standards to guide overarching decisions. People in the district appear to make decisions in isolation. Time will be needed to consider the type of standards and outcomes that will best serve learners. The long-term consequences are tremendous, and planning should not be superficial.

Mapping's big picture affords the opportunity to consider both small-scale and large-scale steps to improve student performance. When it is clear to the faculty and administration that a major area of work needs significant research, the site-based curriculum cabinet should set up a task force to investigate a range of potential solutions. A task force might outline two or three different assessment series for writing between elementary and middle school; three or four different scheduling and teaming configurations for the 9th grade interdisciplinary program; and two different ways to review potential standards and outcomes that have been successful in similar districts. With a range of options on the table, a group is more likely to stay flexible and arrive at an optimum solution.

Traditional curriculum committees can be replaced with lively, strategic investigations based on the authentic data available through mapping. My experience is that people like these groups. They feel real and purposeful rather than bureaucratic and boring.

Phase 7: The Review Cycle Continues

Curriculum review should be active and ongoing. Our old-style method of reviewing curriculum is well intended but odd. Frequently, schools and districts have five-year reviews of a designated subject area, which smacks of a pro forma approach rather than one generated out of real need. And when we take into account the rapid growth in any domain, the idea of a five-year review seems antiquated. Science changes weekly. New literature emerges constantly. Technology is growing at breakneck speed. It is strange that a curriculum area is reviewed at the arbitrary five-year point. I believe this practice emerged because there were no viable alternatives. The technology available was pencil and paper, typewriters, and maybe a few word processors. But now we have a means for ongoing, systematic, immediate, and long-range planning.

With the increase in genuine communication, refinement of curriculum is a real possibility. The next chapter describes the specific tasks and opportunities that each member of a faculty can employ with an initial draft of a curriculum map.

✦   ✦   ✦

3

Reviewing, Analyzing, and Developing Curriculum Maps

A curriculum map is like a school's manuscript. It tells the story of the operational curriculum. With this map in hand, staff members can play the role of manuscript editors, examining the curriculum for needed revision and validation.

This chapter describes six tasks faculty members can carry out with maps to create a workable, vibrant, overall picture of the curriculum. While reviewing the map, faculty members can gain information about ongoing work throughout the building, identify curricular gaps, find repetitions, target potential areas for integration, match assessment with standards, and review for timeliness.

Task 1: Read Maps to Gain Information

As educators, we are only as effective as what we know. If we have no working knowledge of what students studied in previous years, how can we build on their learning? If we have no insight into the curriculum in later grades, how can we prepare learners for future classes? Reading and examining curriculum maps enables us to create a database for making important decisions.

17

At a minimum, if mapping is used to simply find out what is really being taught in a building, staff members are better off than they were without maps. It is always a striking experience when a school staff first reviews maps. It's common to hear colleagues tell each other, "I didn't know you taught that!"

Students are the prime beneficiaries of even a simple read-through of maps. Staff members find that maps expand their perspective and increase the quality of their educational decisions. A curriculum map provides a powerful context for many different people: a grade level team dropping a unit of study, a high school department changing its reading list, a media specialist ordering software, or a new teacher beginning work at a school.

It is crucial to have a broad audience for any read-through of maps. It is tempting only to look at the map of a colleague who deals with similar situations, such as a grade-level teammate or a fellow department member. This kind of communication is certainly important, but the most revealing work occurs when educators read the maps of teachers several grades away or in departments with which they rarely have contact. All students deal daily and through the years with all teachers in a building—although the teachers themselves do not always interact with each other.

Task 2: Identify Gaps

We often assume that all teachers within a discipline address the same curriculum. This isn't always the case. We frequently find gaps between goals and what is actually taught, and these gaps can have a lasting impact on a child's learning. If a middle school science teacher wrongly assumes that entering 6th graders have studied basic physics concepts pertaining to force—and then proceeds to build lessons on those concepts—students might get lost. There is probably a good reason why the 5th grade teachers did not address force, and communication between teachers is obviously critical for the sake of the learner.

Appendix III contains an elementary science map with corresponding skills showing a sequence from kindergarten through 8th grade. It was used to identify and address gaps in a program. Such vertical articulation of the curriculum fosters smoother transitions for students as they move toward secondary school programs.

Coordinators and supervisors cannot and should not be expected to know what transpires in each classroom. It is unrealistic to expect them to interview and observe every classroom teacher with ongoing regularity. Instead, we need to recognize that the operational curriculum committee is composed of each and every classroom teacher in the building (see Chapter 6). The maps they study will reveal missing pieces in vertical and horizontal articulation: years past, years to come, and in the current year. With these data, gaps in content, skills, and assessment can be identified.

Task 3: Identify Repetitions

Too often, teachers assume that they are introducing a book or concept to students for the first time. In fact, many units are repeated over the course of a student's K–12 experience. Maps can reveal such repetition, showing where the same novel or unit is repeatedly addressed.

It is curious to hear teachers defend the teaching of *Sarah, Plain and Tall* in the 4th grade and then again in 7th, or to hear 8th and 9th grade English teachers rationalize *Romeo and Juliet* being taught two years in a row. There are so many other novels and plays to present to young readers! I have heard a teacher claim that he "does the book differently," but this is questionable since it is unlikely that the 4th grade teacher speaks with the 7th grade teacher to be certain they're each taking a unique approach. It also is questionable to justify a district's five units on the rain forest and six units on dinosaurs with the need for "review."

Maps reveal not only content repetitions but also skill repetitions, which should be distinguished from skill spiraling. Without question, students need to practice, review, and drill skills, but they should do so only in the spirit of working toward more complex mastery of those skills. Redundant drill of skills is inherently boring and insulting to the learner, and it is one of the most effective methods for turning students off to learning.

Of greater concern is the repetition of assessments. It is worrisome to see high school students working on reports when their counterparts in 3rd grade also write reports. Too often the "reports" are fundamentally the same request: a summary and identification of key factual information on a topic. I have even seen the same length requirement for both primary and secondary levels. High school students should work on developmentally appropriate assessments (see Chapter 5). Instead of reports, they should create legal briefs, position papers, critiques, original research, action plans, and other outcomes that imitate what will be asked of them throughout their adult lives.

It is the educator's job to study a curriculum map and recommend whether the content, skills, and assessments it details are to be validated or revised. While purposeful spiraling of skill and knowledge is a necessity, needless repetition is a waste of everyone's time.

Task 4: Identify Potential Areas for Integration

When appropriate, merging concepts from two or more disciplines can make for a powerful and lasting learning experience. By perusing the maps for potential linkages among subject matter, teachers discover possibilities for interdisciplinary units of study. Whether the focus is a topic, theme, issue, or problem-based study, elementary and secondary teachers can use maps to find natural connections that will expand and underscore students' learning.

Figure 3.1 shows a continuum of options for selecting the degree and nature of integration (Jacobs 1989), which can help curriculum designers choose the most fruitful type of content delivery system. As individual teachers or team members look over their maps, they can determine which option best serves their learners. Perhaps working directly through a discipline will be the most powerful. This is certainly true when we give the disciplines true integrity, so that students act as "scientists" rather than simply study "science."

FIGURE 3.1
CONTINUUM OF OPTIONS FOR CONTENT DESIGN

Discipline Based	Parallel Disciplines	Multi-Disciplinary	Interdisciplinary Units/Courses	Integrated Day	Complete Program

Another option is to reconfigure when mutually compatible subjects or units are taught so that they run concurrently. A study on statistics and demographics could be resequenced to run in a parallel discipline format with a unit on immigration in social studies. In this instance, teachers are not cowriting the unit; they are coplanning for optimum timing. If, however, the teachers wish to collaborate on the design of a unit and integrate two or more disciplines, then the option is interdisciplinary. At their best, these integrated units are designed around a common organizational structure such as essential questions, which connect key concepts shared by the various disciplines (see Chapter 5).

Not all disciplines need to be involved in the design of a unit, just those that seem applicable. Common examples are humanities studies or math and science fusions. In one 9th grade global studies program, an English teacher, a social studies teacher, and an art teacher have collaborated on a unit of study of Japan and its people. Other disciplines need not participate if their perspective is not naturally applicable, thus making it a multidisciplinary design. Another teacher designed a 2nd grade unit on weather to have primarily a science focus, with opportunities for measurement in mathematics. Interdisciplinary units also can incorporate a wide array of all disciplines. The point is that interdisciplinary designs are best when sensible, not strained, integration is planned.

Educators who wish to have their students initiate and select the total focus for a study might choose a student-centered option, whether in a primary classroom or a senior independent project. In the previous examples, teachers packaged the disciplines around concepts, topics, themes, problems, or issues. With the Integrated Day, the student's problems and points of fascination are the focus.

Setting-based integration describes an environment that is integrated into the study. The learner leaves the classroom walls behind and centers learning on that environment whether it is a school-to-work program, a field study at a conservation area, or a museum trip. The program is a complete integration of the learner in a specific place and time.

When groups are just starting to work in teams, the curriculum map can become a unifying agent. The many opportunities for interdisciplinary work become evident when teachers look at the map, considering what is taught, when it is taught, the concurrent teaching of subjects, and the interplay of skill development among disciplines. Sensible integration is a natural outgrowth of mapping.

Task 5: Match Assessment with Standards

We need evidence of learning to find out if we are effectively meeting our targeted goals for students. The only evidence we have is in what they write, what they say, what they build, what they design, and what they compute—not what we cover. The thoughtful rethinking of assessment has swept the United States as we prepare our children for a more demanding world. Focusing on assessment through the course of the year deepens accountability. For example, if a school is attempting to fulfill a state standard in mathematics, then from September to June, what do students perform and produce that gives evidence of meeting that standard?

Both tangible products and observed performances can serve as the basis for assessing student growth (Jacobs 1996). Whenever major benchmark assessments or cumulative portfolio collections are gathered, there should be a corresponding notation on the map. For example, if a middle school team collects writing samples across the disciplines for a portfolio collection and formally reviews them every eight weeks, the map should show the eight-week marker for monitoring progress.

This task is of particular note because of the current focus on standards. Currently, standards in the United States are being established on four levels: one level is national, primarily through professional organizations representing curricular areas; the second level is state, as seen through state frameworks and standards; the third level is district and school, as each local site translates the national and state standards to its unique community; and the fourth level is the most critical, the classroom, where the operationalization of all standards occur.

It is in the classroom that the student and the standard meet. Mapping becomes the monitoring device to check whether there is sufficient evidence to match a standard in the classroom. The reverse is true as well. Without evidence through student assessment, the standard is a shell. In a sense, the two together complete the equation.

Task 6: Review for Timeliness

With the constant proliferation of knowledge, all who create curriculum maps must update their plans vigilantly. Every day brings new books, ideas, technology, and breakthroughs to the classroom. As teachers scrutinize their maps, they should look for dated materials and possible replacements.

Timeliness also deals with examining the map for best current practice. There are new breakthroughs in all fields of pursuit including education. As a teacher learns a new strategy, he or she should place this strategy on the map. When teachers add the writing process to their repertoire, there will be obvious changes in the assessment section of the map.

By editing, shaping, and adding to our curriculum, there is a genuine sense of collaboration in a school. Stagnation is replaced by growth. With a map there is also an opportunity for refining work, where we go deeper into the curriculum. Rather than simply stating the title of a unit, we can declare the focus and purpose of the unit through essential questions, which are described in the next chapter.

✧　　　✧　　　✧

4

Refining the Map
Through Essential Questions

Navigators use maps to chart a course. Although unforseen events and variables may affect their journey, they begin by making important choices about their route to avoid a meandering, rudderless voyage. In similar fashion, teachers must make critical choices as they plot a course for their learners. *Essential questions* are an exceptional tool for clearly and precisely communicating the pivotal points of the curriculum.

To refine is to improve by introducing distinctions. Curriculum maps provide a natural format for such refinement. By employing essential questions, curriculum makers upgrade the quality of their plans. This chapter defines the nature of essential questions, identifying the kinds of questions that are valuable for refining and organizing the curriculum in the individual classroom and throughout the school. It underscores the value of rewriting a map by using essential questions.

What Is an Essential Question?

An essential question is the heart of the curriculum. It is the essence of what you believe students should examine and know in the short time they have with you.

Ted Sizer's classic work *Horace's Compromise* (1984) was a breakthrough in revealing the daily routine of a teacher grappling with conceptual priorities being consumed day in and day out by nonessential, frivolous lessons. Essential questions can help combat this phenomenon.

If your 6th graders are about to embark on a study of the U.S. Constitution for four weeks, as a curriculum writer you need to ask, "What are the most important concepts that my students should investigate about the Constitution in our four weeks? What should they remember and reflect on a year from now?" In his provocative article "The Futility of Trying to Teach Everything of Importance," Grant Wiggins (1989) points out that we often avoid the heart of the curriculum and cover the periphery. When this happens, learners fail to see the essential purpose of their learning and simply complete tasks because "they're supposed to." Student assessments should focus on essential learning, not merely a task for its own sake.

The essential question is just that: a question. The interrogative suggests investigation and inquiry rather than the more militaristic and directive term "objective." When the curriculum is formed around questions, the clear message to the students is that you are probing with them. Compare a 6th grade class examining "How is the Constitution the backbone structure of America?" to a topical study beginning with the objective: "The student will look at the three branches of the government as organized in the Constitution." Typical Roman numeral outline approaches to curriculum do not engage learners in inquiry; rather, they imply preset answers.

The essential question also is an organizer. To structure an array of activities, it's wise to group activities under essential questions similar to chapter headings in a book. In this way, you can avoid the common "potpourri" problem, which is the random assortment of well-intended activities with no structure (Jacobs 1989).

The potpourri problem plagues many curriculums. Imagine being a 5th grade student about to study ancient Egypt. You have little or no background on the subject. The teacher runs you through a set of activities with no backbone or reference points. You study a little on the Nile, a little on the Egyptian gods and myths, a little on the pyramids, a little on Egyptian irrigation tools, a little on some pharaohs, and a little on some key events. You have received a curricular smorgasbord rather than a cohesive experience. And as a 5th grader, you need all the help you can get to organize your readings and activities! A set of essential questions offer focus throughout a unit of study.

The essential question is a creative choice. Just as an author wrestles with the choice of words in a sentence or a title, so does the creative curriculum writer. With the slightest change, a pedestrian question can become thought provoking. A question such as, "What was the effect of the Civil War?" can be revised to, "Is the Civil War still going on?"

This does not mean that every question has to be clever. In fact, simple questions can be very provocative to children. In the unit on Flight featured in *Interdisciplinary Curriculum: Design and Implementation* (Jacobs 1989), the first question was, "What flies?" Students pursued the question identifying everything from birds, bees, fish, and space shuttles to the notion that time flies and ideas fly. The key is that you create a question of genuine perplexity to the learner.

The essential question is conceptual commitment. When a teacher or group of teachers selects a question to frame and guide curricular design, it is a declaration of intent. In a sense you are saying, "This is our focus for learning. I will put my teaching skills into helping my students examine the key concept implicit in the essential question." Given the limited time you have with your students, curriculum design has become more and more an issue of deciding what you won't teach as well as what you will teach. You cannot do it all. As a designer, you must choose the essential.

The essential question is a skill to be encouraged in students, too. Learners of all ages should be encouraged to raise and to consider essential questions. Children enter kindergarten bursting with questions. Some are offbeat: Why aren't there purple eyes? Others are direct and personal: Teacher, why do you look ugly today? Still others are probing: Why aren't there any dinosaurs around anymore? An early learner's questions are essential to him or to her; there is nothing coy about them. These students are not out to impress the teacher with their questions; they ask readily about everything.

As children get older, they ask fewer and fewer essential questions and more and more managerial or mundane questions. By early adolescence, we hear too many variations on this question from students: Teacher, is this what you want? The modeling of question formation is central to teaching question formation. In the elementary years, students can make judgements about different kinds of questions and their inherent value. Children can learn to recognize, appreciate, and generate essential questions.

How Can Essential Questions Serve as a Scope and Sequence?

The term "scope and sequence" is applied in a variety of ways in curriculum planning. It can be used to describe the scope and sequence of skills and concepts being targeted as key objectives for a subject for the year. For example, educators might refer to the scope and sequence of skills in mathematics for 2nd graders. A history teacher in a high school might refer to the scope and sequence of skills and concepts for a year-long course on Western Civilization. The intention is to provide a blueprint of desired goals. Unfortunately, the language can become stiff and generic in scope and sequence goal statements. For example, statements such as these are more than a little bureaucratic:

- The student will recognize personal responsibility to the community.
- The student will compute two-digit addition operations.
- The student will understand that there is a food chain in each ecosystem.

These statements are not thrilling to young learners—or their teachers for that matter!

I do not challenge the value of these three samples, but I do challenge the language. Given the nature of the task—which is to engage the learner—this is lousy writing. It is better suited to military commands or directions for assembling a file cabinet, where crisp, officious sentences are appropriate. If, as teachers and learners, we can revise these statements into essential questions, we have a much better chance to increase student motivation.

In a humanities unit designed by teachers at a New York City junior high school, these questions were posted for examination:

- How does my community affect my life?
- What do I owe my community? . . . Or do I?

If you were 13 years old, would you rather study these questions or be told that "students will learn to recognize personal responsibility to the community"?

When composing a unit of study for investigation at any level of teaching, creating meaningful and clear essential questions can serve as scope and sequence to the structure of the study. An analogy to the table of contents of a book is apt. Just as the chapter headings in a table of contents describe the scope (range) and the sequence (order) of organization, so do a set of essential questions provide an advanced organizer for a curricular experience. They are the range and parameters of the study. They frame the essence of what your class can realistically examine in the amount of time you have to spend. The questions suggest a logical pattern of investigation through the time ahead for your students, whether it's over the next two weeks or a whole year. The examples in Appendix II underscore the point that no matter what type of curriculum format, age group, or unit length, essential questions focus the learning experience.

What Are Criteria for Writing Essential Questions?

I have distilled the following list of criteria from hundreds of teachers around the country. The list suggests best writing practices for generating essential questions that will guide your learners and refine your teaching.

1. Each child should be able to understand the question. The essential questions are ultimately for your students. If the learner cannot understand the language of the questions, then the purpose is defeated. Sometimes we adults get carried away with our polysyllabic syntax. An example of such indulgence is a question a junior high teacher used for his Civil War unit: "What were the intellectual underpinnings of sectionalism?" This is not a question written for your average 7th grader. Simple sounding questions do not necessarily connote simple answers. In a 1st grade unit on snow, the teachers declared the first essential question as: "What is snow?" The question lent itself to a range of activities from looking at the snow cycle to considering the difference between natural snow and artificial snow made at ski resorts. In short, questions should be clear to your students.

2. The language of the questions should be written in broad, organizational terms. The questions are umbrella-like organizers and should reflect a heading for the focus of a set of activities. Consider the following question from a unit on ancient Greece: "What were the major contributions of the Ancient Greeks?" This makes clear to the learner that through the completion of many activities, they will learn much about the major contributions of the Greeks. However, a question like "What did Socrates have for breakfast?" lacks organizational power. If a question is too specific, it is probably an activity itself or the point of a classroom discussion.

3. The question should reflect your conceptual priorities. The essential question points to the essence of what your students will examine in the course of their study. What is the conceptual priority for them to write about, speak about, think about, and develop? Given the very real limits of time, we must make choices.

The essential question forces the teacher to choose the conceptual outcome for the students. If students negotiate the questions with the teacher, they are choosing as well. In short, if 1st graders examine "What is snow?", the teacher is setting as a conceptual priority an understanding of the nature of snow, its compositions, and its origins.

4. Each question should be distinct and substantial. If a set of questions is akin to a set of chapters in a book, then there should be enough power and substance to hold a "chapter" together. A question such as "What makes a leader?" will require a number of activities and experiences to engage the learner in an investigation. Contrast that with a question like, "What were Franklin D. Roosevelt's favorite books?" Although the question itself might make for an interesting discussion in one class session, it will offer little more than that. The previously cited snow unit for 1st graders had two distinctive essential questions: What is snow? How does snow affect people? This cues students that there will be a set of activities examining the nature of snow and another set examining how snow affects people.

5. Questions should not be repetitious. In my experience, repetitious questions are the most common error in curriculum design. In a unit on the tricentennial celebration of a New England town, the middle school teachers used four essential questions:

- What is change?
- What causes change?
- How does change affect people?
- How has change affected our town over 300 years?

The first three questions were repetitious, which explains the teachers' difficulty in figuring out where to place certain activities. Upon reflection, one of the teachers said, "How can one discuss change without looking at its causes and its impact on people? That's what change is!"

If there are repetitious questions, they should be collapsed into one question with subheads. The questions above were edited to read: What is the nature of change? How has change affected our community? Just as a book chapter should have distinct content integrity, so should each essential question stand on its own without being blurred into another question.

6. The questions should be realistic given the amount of time allocated for the unit or course. This is a pragmatic and critical decision that the designer must weigh. If you have three weeks to spend on a unit on China, the questions will most likely differ in number and kind from a three-month unit on China. It has been my observation that 2 to 5 questions is the average for a unit of study that ranges from 3 weeks to about 12 weeks. Too many questions overwhelm the learner.

7. There should be a logical sequence to a set of essential questions. The test of a good series of questions is that you are able to explain to your students the rationale for the sequence. If that rationale is not clear, learners will likely have problems. The sequence does not have to be rigid. A teacher can move through the questions and return to previous ones. However, the questions should have a sense of focus and direction rather an arbitrary order.

8. The questions should be posted in the classroom. At first this criteria appears to be simply a helpful hint. But it is one of the most crucial variables in predicting long-term retention and understanding on the part of children. Posting the question is a public declaration. The message to the learners is: These questions are essential for you. The questions provide a constant visual organizer and focus for the learner—and for the teacher as well. The questions are a point of reference. When all the teachers participating in an interdisciplinary unit of study post the questions, the students have direct evidence that the teachers are not only talking with each other but share the view that the investigation of these questions is essential.

Seeing is believing. I recommend that teachers wrestle with the design of their units whether discipline based, interdisciplinary, or student centered, and they should focus those studies on essential questions. Curriculum maps in subsequent iterations after the first draft can become clear, precise, and powerful as teachers refine them with essential questions. When a teacher sits at a computer terminal and begins to review his or her maps, a critical and powerful refinement occurs as content is transformed into essential questions.

✧　　　✧　　　✧

5

Using Mapping to Generate Developmental Assessment

In the course of researching curriculum mapping and field-testing its procedures and practices, I noticed a critical problem with assessment. The dilemma was plain when schools accounted for assessments that were to demonstrate content mastery and skill acquisition. I noted remarkable repetitions from kindergarten through grade 12 in the types, or genres, of assessment.

For example, "reports" were listed as a form of assessment for both upper elementary and high school students. Were the high school reports more advanced than the elementary reports? My findings said no. Although subject matter was significantly more advanced for high school students, the type, or genre, was not. In other words, 4th graders are very good at being reporters: finding and organizing information, then reporting it back in their own words (see Figure 5.1 on pp. 37–38). High school students should be doing much more. They should not only work on advanced content but increasingly complex genres as well, such as position papers, argumentative papers, and far more complex reports.

I also noticed that "graphs" and "charts" were on primary curriculum maps as well as high school maps. Again, I found the same result. High school students were frequently producing unidimensional charts that simply compiled data, which is what 1st graders were doing with considerably more enthusiasm.

As Wiggins (1993) points out, we are attempting to assist learners in their quest for understanding at the point in time in which we encounter them in the classroom. Curriculum mapping offers the opportunity to scrutinize our current practice with an eye to the spiraling nature of the learner's experience over time. In fact, the greatest value of mapping comes when teams of teachers review maps to determine the appropriate match between the level of student learning and the type of work expected.

Such reviews often show that an assessment genre is not always a developmental match with the age and stage of the learner. Although the content material of assessment becomes more advanced in higher grades, the genre often does not progress along with it. I propose that developmental genre should match each stage of learning, based on students' characteristics. Figure 5.1 describes these characteristics, which are based on developmental research (Piaget 1932, Lickona 1983, Selman 1980, Kohlberg 1981, Gilligan 1982). I have selected corresponding genres of assessment that match the characteristics. These examples are only a small sampling of the types of work that can be used to match learners with appropriate assessments.

Mapping data concerning the nature of assessment should be edited, audited, and revised to reflect what we know about the learners in our care. Whether the map is at a specific grade level, deals with a set of grade levels at a building, or is districtwide, teachers should become active editors by having a deliberate read-through, scouring for a developmental match between type of assessment and stage. This is a particularly exciting task when there are K–12 maps. If there are only grade-level or building maps because others in your district are not participating, your

FIGURE 5.1
MATCHING LEARNERS AND ASSESSMENT GENRES

K–2 Developmental Characteristics

Cognitive level is concrete operations; sensory-motor modalities dominate; egocentric; parallel play still dominates with the beginning signs of social interaction with other peers; strong need for primary affiliation with a key adult at school and parental surrogates; willingness to experiment and take risks; verbal skills generally more pronounced in girls; spatial-motor generally more pronounced in boys; evident disparities between various areas of development as in fine motor/gross motor differences; uneven development in speaking skills; reading and writing emerges at this level with the learner's fascination with sound-symbol relations.

Examples of K–2 Genres

captions	story boards
labels	story lines
simple research	graphs/charts
maps	joke telling
interview with a key question	observational drawing

Grades 3–5 Developmental Characteristics

Cognitive operations are moving through concrete functions with early signs of simple abstract thinking; students are able to combine several concepts and perceive cause-and-effect relationships; fascination with the world; excellent "reporters" and seekers of interesting information; social skills related strongly to peers and to teachers; enjoys large group projects; social concern for others emerging; physical stability and agility.

Examples of Grade 3–5 Genres

simple research report	extended research report
note cards	interview: question series
short stories	photo essay with text
artifact analysis	comparative observations
newspaper articles	

(continued)

FIGURE 5.1—*(continued)*
MATCHING LEARNERS AND ASSESSMENT GENRES

Grades 6–8 Developmental Characteristics

Labile period of development; surge into formal operations; quest for personal identity; heightened sensitivity to ego and to views of peers; fascination with issues of fairness, justice, and trust; pronounced surges in physical development; uneven development among peers; self-consciousness about physical presence; concern for others conflicting with concern for self.

Examples of Grade 6–8 Genres

persuasive essays	descriptive essays
analytic essays	personal essays
hypothesis testing	issue-based forums
blueprints and models	original play writing
museum text/captions	four note-taking forms

Grades 9–10 and 11–12 Developmental Characteristics

Significant differences among 9th and 12th graders progressing from midadolescent concerns to pre-adult education; formal operations involving abstract concepts; projections; social life focused on smaller groupings and pairings; sexuality is an issue; physical maturity rapidly paces; focus on future and next steps.

Examples of Grades 9–10 and 11–12 Genres

position papers	legal briefs
business plans	anthologies
choreography	game book
film and literary criticism	senior project and defense
work study analysis	interview simulations
case studies	original musical compositions

learners benefit because you have taken the time to improve the quality of their assessment by matching it to their learning stage.

When mapping reveals overlaps in assessment genres at varying grades, it's also useful to examine actual samples of student work. When teachers and administrators can pick up a piece of student writing or handle a project, the visceral contact forces close inspection. It is surprisingly revealing to watch teachers review a variety of student work. On occasion, I have seen high school teachers startled by the realization that they are requesting the exact genre of work as their elementary colleagues. At other times, upper elementary or middle school teachers recognize that they are underserving their learners by not better preparing them for more difficult tasks in the high school.

Examining student work focuses discussion among teachers in a building, grade level, or department. Frequently, there are vast disparities among teachers' expectations in the course of a student's year. For example, when a group of teachers examines the quality and nature of a student's writing among subject areas, they have the chance to clarify the match of the assignment to the stage of the learner. It is always fascinating to see how surprised a science teacher is to find that his students write with more care and precision in English. When examining student work together, teachers also have the chance to consider the commonly held beliefs among their colleagues in areas such as standards of excellence in visual work, spoken performances, and writing.

It also is helpful for teachers to generate additions to the lists cited in Figure 5.1 and to add a descriptive sentence or two to each item. By elaborating on the list of cognitive, social, and physical characteristics of their learners, teachers actively reflect on who their students are, what motivates them, and what they fundamentally need. This activity should be specifically targeted to the population living in the community in which the teachers work. Teachers should consider, for example, the size of the school; whether it is urban, suburban, or rural; whether students are college bound or school-to-work; community values; and family demographics.

Too often we fail to identify specifics about the students we serve. We have a general sense of teaching based on years of experience or what we think we are supposed to ask of learners. With constant changes and shifts in society, we need corresponding adjustments in the way we approach learners. Simply put, additional information apart from developmental considerations is critical to learners' success.

For example, many teachers find they work with an increasingly diverse student population in terms of language skills. It would be wise to consider the types of assessment that take such diversity into account. Another factor that directly affects assessment is the size of a class. Obviously, numbers of students affect the kinds of experiences students can have in the classroom.

As children develop over time, the concept of the spiraling curriculum (Bruner 1966) comes into play. We generate increasingly more complex and demanding skills and concepts for students as they develop and as we build on what has already been taught.

✧   ✧   ✧

6

A Case for Eliminating Curriculum Committees

Whether you're talking about the printing press, slate and chalk, or a computer screen, technological breakthroughs have always created exciting possibilities for students. With each new addition of technology to classroom life, learners adjust and embrace change. It is critical that teachers and administrators approach their professional work with the same spirit of innovation. Curriculum mapping provides an opportunity to reconsider the most fundamental assumptions about curriculum decision making. In particular, the immediate access to information that mapping provides changes the context and basis for developing and refining curriculum and assessment.

The Old Scenario: The Curriculum Committee Meeting

The meeting place is a classroom after school. The teachers file in for the District Science Curriculum Committee. Chosen by their principals for their particular areas of strength, the teachers are to work on a list of skills and objectives to be used with students. The conversation turns toward the type of curriculum and lessons that each teacher has addressed in his or her classroom. This is where reality breaks down.

The charge of the meeting was to "represent" the curricular practice going on in each building. At the table were two elementary representatives from each of four buildings, two science teachers from the middle school, two high school science teachers, and the science department chair. In reality, no matter how competent these instructors may be, it is virtually impossible for them to represent their buildings because *they do not and cannot know what is actually going on in all the classrooms.* Each teacher can only honestly report what is going on in his or her own classroom.

Take, for example, the two elementary representatives. One is a 2nd grade teacher and the other is a 5th grade teacher. They cannot interview every school colleague to report what is going on in the school. So when the discussion at the meeting turns to the elementary curriculum, these two representatives talk about what they know, which is basically their own classrooms. They report a narrow view of what's really happening at that school.

Ultimately, the most hazardous result of these kinds of meetings is that decisions about what will be taught are decided in the vacuum of the subject area without deliberate regard for any other subject. The outcome of this situation is evidenced, for example, in schools where U.S. literature is taught sophomore year and U.S. history taught junior year. Not only does this prevent the sensible integration of content areas, but teachers lose the opportunity to integrate skills across disciplines and assessments.

Teachers could link many more assignments, experiences, lessons, and plans for their learners if they had needed information readily available. Curriculum maps make that possible. It is not that department meetings should be thrown off the school agenda; rather, we should refocus their purpose. The vertical curriculum is dependent on the horizontal plane of work as well. If teachers had more opportunities to be deliberate about the overall design of curriculum, they could merge and reinforce key concepts, skills, and assessment.

Curriculum mapping on the macro level provides three assets to the design process that can and should alter curriculum decision making: immediate access to data, analytic and sorting possibilities, and ease in communicating with others.

Imagine our aforementioned curriculum committee meeting with mapping data at hand. The chair could readily obtain a printout of the operational curriculum from all four elementary schools in addition to any other subject areas. The middle school teacher could consider a realistic view of the transition between the elementary and middle school program in science. Interdisciplinary possibilities open up as the high school and middle school teachers rethink the horizontal sweep of the curriculum. The committee would discuss what people actually are doing in classrooms, not what others think they are doing.

Perhaps the key word "rain forest" is put into the computer to find all places in the school curriculum where that subject is taught. Working from curriculum maps, the computer identifies seven places K–12 where the keyword appears. Or, in a quest to improve speaking skills and research skills, a district task force enters the key word "interviewing skills." The computer identifies numerous responses, with the first one in 3rd grade. With the advent of standards, teachers in a building may want to search the district map for a type of assessment such as "bar graphs" to see if they are developed with sufficient complexity from elementary through high school mathematics classes.

There is always the real possibility that the computer might identify no entries for a particular key word. This highlights a glaring gap. If a task force finds nothing on the key words "critical thinking and television," they've now identified an area for development.

For years we've lacked the power of an overarching context for making curriculum decisions. The information that would inform decisions has been lacking or impossible to collect and understand. We ignore stacks of curriculum guides that are written in lists of desired objectives that infrequently represent reality; when we use them, they can actually distort a decision. Calendar-based mapping is a new and very practical alternative.

If Not Committees, Then What?

Buried in the word committee is the word commit. It is noteworthy that there are three starkly different meanings of the word. One deals with devotion and perseverance. Another suggests carrying out and executing tasks for good or negative purposes (committing a crime). The third meaning deals with confinement and institutionalization.

Implicit in these three definitions is an answer to why so many schools and district committees don't work effectively. It is the confining nature of the committee that prevents a group of genuinely devoted individuals from carrying out meaningful tasks. My hunch is that the majority of curriculum committees are in place because they have always been there. When actions are institutionalized, they also become routine and automatized. This is not to say that curriculum committees haven't had successes, but their fundamental design has inherent problems.

To replace the cumbersome style of curriculum committees, I propose replacements based on ideas from site-based management, organizational psychology, systems theory, and observations from the field. The core element, however, is the necessary database available on a curriculum map accessible to all parties through technology.

Organization of Councils, Cabinets, and Task Forces

To provide a more powerful and worthwhile means of determining curriculum decisions, I advocate replacing departmental curriculum committees with a four-part scheme.

1. Each school consists of individual teachers. All teachers participate in mapping. In effect, all teachers are operational curriculum developers. Included in this

group are related areas where curriculum is sometimes directly and indirectly affected, such as guidance counselors, librarians, media specialists, and health professionals.

Using calendar-based curriculum maps, each teacher enters the operational curriculum on the computer. It is the most critical of all responsibilities because ultimately it is the classroom where content, skills, and assessment are developed. The only professional who can accurately report about what is going on in a building is the classroom teacher.

2. If a teacher has a specific concern or need, this should be presented to his or her representative to the *site-based curriculum council* (see Figure 6.1). The council is composed of teachers and staff members representing all parts of the school program. The elementary school may have representatives who will serve both primary and upper elementary classrooms, special area teachers, special education, media specialists, and guidance. Secondary schools may elect to have representatives from teams, departments, divisions, special areas, special education, guidance, and media as well. Of particular note is the potential role of the library media specialist, who can serve as a turn key to the mapping process (Eisenberg and Johnson 1996). The media specialist has access to the most concentrated resource center for supporting the curriculum. Frequently, media specialists are comfortable with computers and can assist reluctant colleagues. With his or her close connection to technology and to all faculty members, the library media specialist holds a pivotal position in map development.

The site-based curriculum council should consider critical points from all teachers regarding mapping review; coordinate school-based efforts to collect data for curriculum mapping; negotiate points of dispute among teachers, departments, and teams regarding content, skill, and assessment; and present the school's point of view at districtwide sessions. It is important to note that any classroom teacher can attend a council meeting if the agenda is pertinent to him or her.

FIGURE 6.1
SITE-BASED CURRICULUM COUNCIL

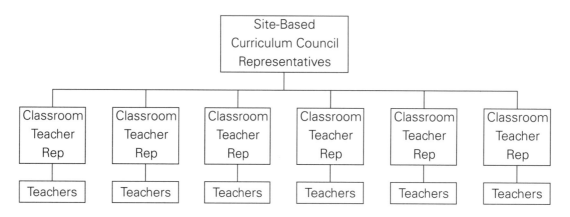

3. The coordination of important districtwide work is handled through the *district curriculum cabinet* (or schoolwide cabinet if the district is a single building, single campus, or private institution). All the representatives from various sites and levels send their subgroup to represent the site at periodic cabinet level meetings, as illustrated in Figure 6.2.

FIGURE 6.2
AT THE DISTRICT LEVEL

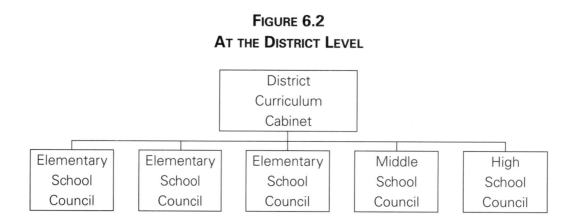

The relationship between sites is based on feeder patterns between schools (see Figure 6.3). In other words, issues of coordination should focus on those areas directly relevant to the flow of students between buildings. For example, if there are troublesome differences between elementary schools that affect students entering the middle school, then the cabinet should address the disparities.

The role of the district curriculum cabinet is similar to that of an editor-in-chief at a publishing house. The editor-in-chief does not write the books in a series but examines them to make sure there are no major gaps and that transitions are clear. In the same spirit, the cabinet is only concerned with issues that have districtwide implications—not areas that are clearly a site-based matter. The cabinet should review the overall map and anticipate initiatives that will affects students as they move between and among buildings.

FIGURE 6.3
RELATIONSHIP BETWEEN SCHOOL COUNCILS

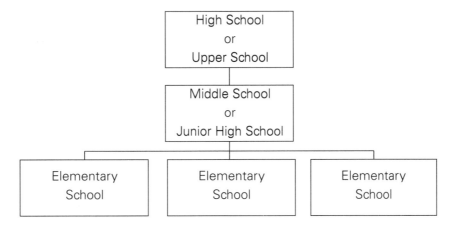

4. When the cabinet sees the need for intensive study or development, it puts together a *district task force* (see Figure 6.4). A site-based council could also set up a building task force if needed. In both instances, the task force will only work on a specific area of need. For example, if one of the elementary schools wants to examine the purchase of math manipulatives K–5 in its building, it can create a task force for that purpose. When the purchase is completed and evaluated, the task force can be disbanded. In this case there was no need for a district-level intervention, though

other elementary schools may be interested in the purchase as might the receiving middle school.

FIGURE 6.4
DISTRICT TASK FORCES

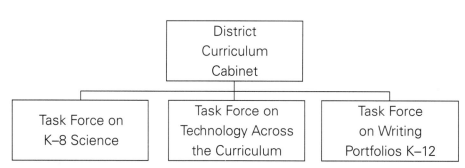

If a task force is concerned about the quality of writing as revealed on performance assessment across subject areas and at all levels of instruction, then a district writing task force would be established with specific purposes, functions, and goals. An action plan is a critical aspect of any task force and would be necessary here.

In short, educators should go to meetings when there is a need, a purpose, and an informed context in which to make appropriate decisions. I believe that data from a curriculum map coupled with teacher and administrative curriculum planning teams at four levels is a viable means of replacing one of the vestiges of the late 1800s—the curriculum committee.

✧   ✧   ✧

7

Practitioners Talk About Making Maps

Over the past decade, I have been fortunate to work with many school administrators and teachers who have implemented curriculum mapping. In this chapter, a few of them share their insights and suggestions. They speak candidly about issues that arise during mapping, offer recommendations about the process, and testify to the broad perspective that mapping provides.

Mapping at a Southern Urban Magnet School

The Chattanooga School for the Liberal Arts is a K–8 magnet school in an urban system in Tennessee. Mary Ann Holt, the school's director, shares her perspective on curriculum mapping.

> Curriculum mapping gave us an opportunity to reflect on what was being taught, the way we were teaching, and where our problems were. An integrated map is posted outside each classroom for visitors, parents, and interested parties to view. We consider these maps works in progress and expect them to change and grow as we change and grow.
>
> Mapping is an ongoing process that is worthy of time. Once the teachers "let go" and got into discussions, interest grew. The ownership by the teachers

is powerful. Talk around the school is rich and reflective. In every instance where an issue was raised on the map, teachers negotiated . . . for the best developmental placement of concepts and skills. They traded materials and ideas for units. Our essential question for the development of each domain was: "When a child enters our school in kindergarten and leaves after 8th grade, what will he/she know in each domain or strand when he/she leaves?"

The maps are now on disks. Each teacher has a complete disk and makes changes as the team's curriculum changes. We found it helpful to make changes at the semester break. These disks are recopied at the end of each year. We look for natural places for integration. Since teachers had negotiated the domain maps, the integrated maps moved quickly. Teachers liked the idea of using broad concepts as a "header" so forced integration of a subject would not be an issue. (Please refer to our 5th grade map in Appendix III.)

It must be noted here that teachers began to plan with our media specialist (as a result of mapping). This enabled her not only to pull materials for units but to order needed materials and have them on hand before the unit was to begin. This also provided teachers with another collaborative colleague. The classroom teacher and the media specialist were both able to see the picture of the entire school and to naturally work library research skills into the curriculum.

Let's not forget the important factor: the kids! We involve the students in preplanning the unit. We use "KWL." The K is, "What do you know about the proposed unit?" The W is, "What do you want to know?" The L is, "What have you learned at its completion?"

At Chattanooga we believe curriculum mapping to be a powerful and logical vehicle for teacher reflection and for parent understanding of what we do with their children.

Mapping in a Suburban District Engaged in Reform

Another perspective on mapping is offered by high school principal Jim Coffey of Mamaroneck High School in suburban Westchester County, New York.

Curriculum mapping disproves the Vermont farmer's adage that you can't get there from here. In fact, mapping clearly defines both here and there. Two years ago my high school launched a major initiative to create a 9th grade interdisciplinary humanities team for all freshman. Fortuitously, we worked with Heidi (Jacobs), who helped us create curriculum maps in English and history. For the first time this group of talented teachers saw clearly the natural intersecting points in the curriculum, which collaboration and mapping provided.

Since U.S. classrooms are often monuments to isolation, encouraging true collaboration among teachers is indeed challenging. Curriculum mapping is a wonderfully nonthreatening point of entry for conversations about curriculum. It is nonjudgmental and invites free discussion of what-is-not and what-might-be.

For those schools that embark on a curriculum mapping project, it would be wise to begin with one area of the curriculum or a particular discipline. Managing a whole school initiative at the same time can be overwhelming and may unintentionally diminish the process. It is also important to have the faculty create a sense of ownership about the need for curriculum mapping. A faculty that has been struggling with essential questions about its programs and direction will more readily embrace the concept of curriculum mapping. A school that is attempting to answer what students should know before they graduate and how it will assess that is an ideal candidate for the rich conversations surrounding a curriculum mapping project.

This school's work with mapping has been sensible and open, encouraging dialogue, debate, and lively interaction by all parties. With Jim's encouragement and editorial input, I wrote a set of questions and answers to acquaint faculty members, parent groups, and the larger community with mapping. You also may be able to use that information, found in Appendix I.

Mapping in a Large New England District

There are several layers of consideration when districts take on mapping as a focus for improving student performance and teacher growth. Carol Perotta, assistant superintendent of the West Hartford Public Schools in Connecticut, shares her experience with what she calls "solving the curriculum puzzle." With her staff, she orchestrated a decision-making structure that encourages active faculty participation at both the school and district level.

Embarking on a program to overhaul the West Hartford Public School curriculum, administrators and teachers alike discovered that the most versatile and consistently useful tool in their possession was the curriculum map. In order to discover what the district needed in terms of curriculum work, we formed the district Curriculum Cabinet, a body of representatives from the Board of Education; the Curriculum Office; and each of the elementary, middle, and high schools. Building-level curriculum planning teams were formed at each site. These teams, made up of representatives to the Curriculum Cabinet, have been highly influential in making decisions about the curriculum. Both the Cabinet and the teams found the maps a critical element in the process of curriculum development.

Maps are created at the beginning of each year by teachers and are reviewed periodically throughout the year to assess the success of the curriculum. All subjects are mapped for essential understandings and essential skills to be gained by students in the designated time period—plus activities for accomplishing the goals and assessment methods. Also included are possible points of integration between subjects or with special area teachers, field studies, or other events.

This last point is one of the advantages to mapping. Consider a 4th grade teacher focusing on the question "What is history?", primarily a social studies topic. Relevant activities include a visit from a local historian and completion of students' oral histories. The teacher expands into other disciplines by overlapping the theme with reading/literature, choosing a work of historical fiction such as one by Laura Ingalls Wilder. Likewise, a journal writing activity entitled "Describing a Hiding Place" encourages students to explore personal history while developing writing skills. A middle school example based on the theme of space includes math/science activities that explore such concepts as circumference, weight, gravity, and time. Tying the theme to literature, students read science fiction or biographies of astronauts. A multicultural/historical perspective is added through the study of Native American, Greek, Roman, and Chinese mythologies and views of the universe. Opportunities for integration among disciplines are easily targeted as teachers refine their curriculum maps.

Teachers have found the curriculum maps to be beneficial in other ways as well. One teacher remarked that they are an excellent time line. A new teacher indicated that the maps helped her feel confident that she was in line with more experienced teachers. Others also expressed the confidence they felt knowing their work could be justified by the map. Teachers appreciate the flexibility of maps; they serve as a guide for the year but can be revised as needed, with room to comment for future reference. One elementary art teacher found that perusing the maps of other teachers helped her to devise art projects that tied in with classroom activities, thus going beyond the integration already provided in the art curriculum. Finally, mapping allows for a consistent districtwide curriculum for all grades, promoting equality between schools.

For curriculum planning, maps reveal a wealth of information. Gaps in the content become evident, and repetitions also are easily spotted. With teacher input, decisions to address gaps and repetitions are based on both developmental ability and proper sequencing.

Curriculum development is an ongoing process of evaluation, a continuous effort to incorporate new technologies, research, and methodologies into the overall scheme, even as the goal remains constant: a curriculum that prepares our students to reach the highest standards. Curriculum maps are the tools of the practitioner, the foundation upon which other work is based.

Mapping, a Middle School English Teacher, and Technology

A different angle on mapping comes from Werner Liepolt, a middle school English teacher from Westport, Connecticut. He also is an instructor at Teachers College, Columbia University, and works with Apple Computer. I met Werner a number of years ago when I was asked to speak about mapping with the faculty at Westport Public Schools. I mentioned that a software program for mapping would be of great value to teachers. Werner and his colleague Bob Matsuoka worked persistently on a software program called The Cartographer to make the mapping process efficient and effective for teachers (Liepolt and Matsuoka 1993); see also http://www.cmap. com. Here, Werner comments on that software.

> Designing what became The Cartographer involved restating my idea as a problem. I needed to break the problem in two. How to get the curriculum mapping information into the computer—and how to get the information out. Information in the three categories of content, skills, and assessment had to be organized by time. At first I thought we might organize the school year by semester or quarters, but we decided to tag the information by calendar month. After all, the year the rest of the world follows is organized that way.

> Teachers had to be able to see the curriculum mapping tool easily. I know teachers with doctorates who have trouble using a word processor. The mapping tool had to be easier than a word processor. No margin settings, no tab setting to interfere with the flow of information. Only those text enhancements that were necessary: boldface, underlining and italics for indicating book titles, and the like.

> Educators were to record their professional work. I wanted them to use the computer with a minimum of training. Intimidation would undoubtedly halt the process. At some point during the early process, someone suggested that a secretary could be trained to enter the curriculum map information from what teachers wrote by hand, that I didn't have to strive so hard to make it easy for every teacher to use. I balked at the idea because curriculum mapping is very much a matter of ownership, and what enhances ownership is the teacher. . .using the computer tool. Teachers who have put their curriculum maps into The Entry tool of The Cartographer can review their work, change, upgrade, and update their maps when they will. Additionally, teachers who have written their own curriculum maps into The Cartographer will have that experience to refer to as they plan how best to integrate technology into their curriculum.

With great care and craftsmanship, Werner and Bob model the best of the 21st century educator. They employed technology to assist their colleagues in dynamic curriculum reform. However, mapping can begin whether teachers are comfortable with technology or not, whether computers are available or not.

For teachers who have no background in technology or no access to computers, simply using a large sheet of butcher paper posted on a wall might be the place to start. I have worked with teachers using different colored markers to represent different subjects or types of data (content, skills, and assessment). The highly visible presence of the marked-up butcher paper is a vibrant worksheet for the entire faculty to use. My first experiences with mapping in the '70s and '80s occurred with middle school teachers coming to work sessions with their curriculum handwritten on large index cards. We spread these cards out on a long table in the library with the months of the year, rearranged them, and edited them.

I advocate technology simply to point out the benefits that a computer database can offer education professionals. If teachers feel inexperienced with computers but are willing to try entering their data, it's an obvious choice to offer software programs to the majority of the staff. Many schools have individuals who are technology experts, or at least have advanced skills in that area. I have seen several schools and districts support these people in developing a format for implementation of curriculum mapping. It makes sense to use a familiar database such as Hypercard for MAC users, Clarisworks for MAC or Windows, or ACCESS or EXCEL from Windows-based Microsoft Office. Other schools have brought in outside agencies to develop programs such as The Cartographer. The key point is to reassure educators that mapping is a straightforward process, whether it's on computer or with pen and paper.

Mapping in a Rural Regional District

Lyn Haas, associate superintendent, offers important insights into the question of how best to begin mapping. Lyn was responsible for initiating and carrying out mapping in the Windsor-Southwest Supervisory Union in southern Vermont. Teachers representing the many rural schools that dot the New England landscape came together under Lyn's leadership to lay the groundwork for mapping. Students from a wide range of elementary and middle schools with differing philosophies all ultimately enroll in the Green Mountain Union High School. It was important to establish a common mapping format with the flexibility to adapt to the various school settings.

Actually the way mapping has played out, teachers move through three personal phases that correlate directly with their growth as technology users. In the first phase, the teacher enters his or her data. We found that the most important thing was that the computer program was easily understood by teachers. Frankly, the teacher's comfort level had everything to do with how effectively mapping occurred. I chose to create a simple database using Clarisworks because that is what we all had available. I would encourage school districts to go with a program that will reinforce the (teachers') comfort level.

The second phase of mapping increased with teacher sophistication on the computer. Some of our teachers involved in the mapping project took a course in PIVOT, a software program that is a platform allowing them not only to record their maps but also to showcase the curriculum units, courses, and recommended standards that stand behind every entry. The PIVOT program adds a professional dimension to curriculum work and allows for passing units to other teachers through our computer network.

The third phase that I am seeing now is with a group of teachers commencing work on Scholastic's Electronic Portfolios, with collections of student assessments, products, and performances that we are able to store and to share. This program provides a simple means of storing a vast amount of data on a computer disk.

All three levels focus on the core and power of the K-12 curriculum map. All of the pieces of our program are coming together, sometimes in bits and pieces, and then in sudden bursts as teachers make leaps in their own understanding of technology.

Lyn's commonsense approach to the mapping process was exemplified in many "trial runs" with teacher leaders. They practiced mapping sessions in simulations to prepare for actual meetings at various schools. Never underestimate the importance of comfort to the mapping process.

It is also clear that the very act of using technology for professional purposes encourages teachers to increase their personal awareness of and skill with the computer. A number of administrators and supervisors have shared the observation that mapping positively affects teachers' comfort with technology.

To summarize, map makers offer a number of recommendations about the mapping process.

• Make a clear case for the purpose of mapping based on communication needs. Mapping is not a philosophy. It is a means of finding out the operational curriculum in any setting, whatever the prevailing beliefs might be (see Chapters 1 and 3).

• Consider staff readiness for beginning the process of school improvement. Readiness is important in terms of a desire to upgrade, validate, and revise programs (see Chapter 2 and 7).

• Consider the technological literacy of the staff. Begin with software programs that are easy for all to use. Reassure staff members that mapping is a doable task whether they begin work with paper and pencil or on a simple software program (see Chapter 7).

• Give staff members ample time for interaction during the first year of map making. The first year of data collection is labor intensive. If the scope of the mapping is relatively modest, teachers can often take on the task during planning periods. If the scope involves the entire building, everyone needs time to examine the collected data (see Chapters 2 and 3).

• Rethink the role of district coordination. Award genuine decision-making power to the site-based curriculum councils and the districtwide cabinets. Curriculum maps provide the opportunity to replace existing curriculum structures with better ones (see Chapter 6).

• Stimulate teachers to take basic mapping tasks further as their own skills with technology open up fantastic possibilities. Whether they edit the curriculum for essential questions or developmental assessments, teachers can revise and renew their curriculum (see Chapters 4, 5, and 7).

The suggestions of the educators in this chapter reflect time, work, and thought. Mapping has become a priority for them and for countless others. They wish to increase the capability of teachers and administrators to provide students with more coherent and focused experiences throughout their school experiences.

✧   ✧   ✧

Bibliography

ASCD. (1993). *Integrating the Curriculum* (videotape). Alexandria, Va.: ASCD.

Bruner, J.S. (1966). *Toward a Theory of Instruction.* Cambridge, Mass.: Harvard University Press.

Costa, A., and B. Kallick. (1995). "Through the Lens of a Critical Friend." In *Assessment in the Learning Organization: Shifting the Paradigm,* edited by A. Costa and B. Kallick. Alexandria, Va.: ASCD.

Eisenberg, M., and D. Johnson. (May–June 1996). "Computer Literacy and Information Literacy: A Natural Combination." *Emergency Librarian* 23, 5: 12–16.

English, F.W. (April 1980). "Curriculum Mapping." *Educational Leadership* 37, 7: 558–559.

English, F.W. (1983). "Contemporary Curriculum Circumstances." In *Fundamental Curriculum Decisions,* edited by F.W. English. Alexandria, Va.: ASCD.

Gilligan, C. (1982). *In a Different Voice.* Cambridge, Mass.: Harvard University Press.

Jacobs, H. (1989). *Interdisciplinary Curriculum: Design and Implementation.* Alexandria, Va.: ASCD.

Jacobs, H. (October 1991). "Planning for Curriculum Integration." *Educational Leadership* 49, 2: 27–28.

Jacobs, H. (1996). "Redefining Assessment." In *Social Studies Educator's Handbook,* edited by Marianne Gunderson. Upper Saddle River, N.J.: Prentice Hall.

Kohlberg, L. (1981). *The Philosophy of Moral Development.* San Francisco: Harper and Row.

Lickona, T. (1983). *Raising Good Children.* New York: Bantam Books.

Liepolt, W., and B. Matsuoka. (1993). The Cartographer. (software program). Westport, Conn.: Collaborative Design. (Contact: Collaborative Design, 27 Bridge St., Westport, CT 06880.)

Piaget, J. (1932). *The Moral Judgment of the Child.* Glencoe, Ill.: Free Press.

Selman, R. (1980). *The Growth of Interpersonal Understanding.* New York: Academic Press.

Sizer, T. (1984). *Horace's Compromise: The Dilemma of the American High School.* Boston, Mass.: Houghton Mifflin Company.

Wiggins, G. (November 1989). "The Futility of Trying to Teach Everything of Importance." *Educational Leadership* 47, 3: 44–59.

Wiggins, G. (1993). *Assessing Student Performance: Exploring the Purpose and Limits of Testing.* San Francisco: Jossey-Bass.

Appendix I
Questions and Answers
About Curriculum Mapping

What is curriculum mapping?

Curriculum mapping is a procedure for collecting data about the actual curriculum in a school district using the school calendar as an organizer. Data are gathered in a format that allows each teacher to present an overview of his or her students' actual learning experiences. The fundamental purpose of mapping is communication. The composite of each teacher's map in a building or district provides efficient access to a K-12 curriculum perspective both vertically and horizontally. Mapping is not presented as what *ought* to happen but what *is* happening during the course of a school year. Data offer an overview perspective rather than a daily classroom perspective. Curriculum mapping is an extremely useful tool for creating a "big picture" for curriculum decision making.

Why do curriculum mapping?

Realistic information about the curriculum that learners encounter is essential for decision making. But given the tremendous demands on teachers and schools, it is extremely difficult to gather such data. Even in the same building it is a challenge to find time for discussions among grade levels, departments, and teams. Among buildings, there are virtual Grand Canyons in communication. Integration of curriculum is about vertical planning as well as horizontal planning. Without a context for looking at students' experiences over time, we make isolated decisions. Curriculum mapping addresses all of these challenges.

How can curriculum mapping benefit a school district?

The tremendous value of mapping is that educators at a site can edit, review, validate, and develop curriculum and assessment with confidence and in context. With a K-12 overview of what is actually going on in classrooms, individual teachers can build on previous years with more authenticity and better prepare students for the future. During the course of any school year, teachers in a grade-level or interdisciplinary team can plan more easily and coordinate units of study and activities. Departments can make more cogent decisions because they have better information about what is going on not only within the building but among buildings. A district can match its current assessments with all levels of standards. It is virtually impossible for any one person or committee to stay on top of the curriculum. Mapping provides a direct, honest, and accessible tool to help all parties in the district carry out that task.

What is shown on the map?

Three types of data are collected: a brief description of the content (whether it is student centered, interdisciplinary, or discipline based); a description of the processes and skills emphasized; and the nature of the assessment the student produces as evidence of growth.

Do maps make the curriculum standard and rigid?

No—quite the opposite! Rigidity occurs when communication is weak and revision is cumbersome. Mapping promotes a living curriculum because it deals with real time. Teachers can "tell it like it is" rather than cope with a bureaucratic approach to describing the flow of their classrooms. The possibility for changing and upgrading the curriculum is increased when a map is entered on a computer. Mapping promotes informed autonomy.

Will mapping change the way we make curriculum decisions?

In general, districts find that they rely less on committees and more on site-based curriculum cabinets. Given that it is the school that each student attends, the focus of curriculum planning should be there. The district can best serve learners by coordinating site-based cabinets on issues and questions regarding transitions, benchmarks, and major initiatives with K-12 implications. More time should be spent at the school sites for planning curriculum and assessment. A school site becomes increasingly effective with more reliable data for making functional decisions, and mapping provides that data.

✧　　　✧　　　✧

Appendix II
Sample Essential Questions

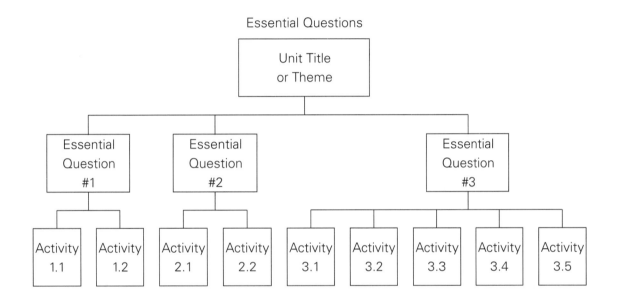

Essential Questions

Flight

- What flies?

- How and why do things in nature fly?

- How does flight impact human beings?

- What is the future of flight?

4th grade, six-week interdisciplinary unit

Intelligence

- What is intelligence?

- How has intelligence evolved?

- How is intelligence measured?

- Is intelligence solely a human phenomenon?

- How will intelligence be altered?

11th grade, four-week A.P. Biology interdisciplinary unit

Multiplication

• How will I ever learn to multiply?

• Where will I ever use multiplication?

2nd and 3rd grade (multigrade classroom), three-week intensive mathematics unit, skills then used throughout the year

Prejudice and Tolerance

• What are the different kinds of human prejudice?

• How can tolerance be taught?

• What has been the impact of individual and group prejudice?

• How can I become more tolerant?

8th grade, three-week interdisciplinary team thematic unit

Everyday Physics: Transportation Safety

• How can cars, boats, and airplanes become safer for passengers?

• How can principles of force and motion help driver effectiveness and safety?

• Are safety and speed compatible?

12th grade, six-week cycle physics course, seminar model

Ancient Egypt: Land of the Pharaohs

• Why Egypt?

• What were major contributions of the ancient Egyptians?

• What is their legacy?

6th grade, seven-week humanities unit, middle school interdisciplinary team unit

Independent Study: Publishing as an Adolescent

• What is the personal story behind my selected adolescent authors?

• How do publishing houses make decisions about submitted manuscripts?

• What is my plan to get published?

• How can I prepare to make a career in publishing?

8th grade, one semester student-centered option

AIDS: A Plague in Our Time

• What is AIDS, and how is it different from other viruses?

• How does AIDS affect the individual?

• How does AIDS affect society?

• What can I do to prevent the spread of this disease?

middle school, two-week intensive schoolwide interdisciplinary unit

Snow

• What is snow?

• How does it affect people?

• How does it affect me?

1st grade, three-week interdisciplinary unit

Japan: Global Studies

• What are the roles of the individual in Japan?

• How does the physical environment of Japan impact its people?

• What is the structure of Japanese society?

• Why Japan?

9th grade, six-week English, social studies, and humanities unit

✧　　　✧　　　✧

Appendix III
Sample Curriculum Maps

This appendix contains samples of many maps showing the variety of ways they can appear and how they can assist you in your school or district. Some of the maps are more detailed than others. Some focus on an individual teacher; others represent a range of teacher input. As you review these pages, keep in mind that you are looking at one map from a school's full complement of maps. When a teacher or principal has access to all of a school's maps, the big picture lifts right off the page.

Map A: Kindergarten Curriculum Map

This map is included because primary grade classrooms are often based on different school day configurations than older grades. (1 page)

Map B: 5th Grade Mathematics Curriculum Map

This map from the Chattanooga School for the Liberal Arts shows the planning that goes into one area of the curriculum. (2 pages)

Map C: 5th Grade Integrated Curriculum Map

Contrasted with the previous map, this 5th grade teacher shows the math curriculum alongside other areas in the curriculum across the school year. The primary emphasis here is on the content entries. (2 pages)

Map D: 8th Grade Humanities Team

The map shows the value of a format that allows several disciplines to integrate content, skills, and assessment. (1 page)

Map E: 9th Grade Interdisciplinary "Life Sciences" Program Map

Teachers devised this map based on major themes for four quarters to convey to students, teachers, and parents an overview of the 9th grade collaboration in health, biology, and physical education. (1 page)

Map F: 11th Grade Science Map

This map reflects the planning of a high school science teacher who has some assessments that run throughout the year, as indicated with arrows and other more focused assessments. (1 page)

Map G: K–8 Science Curriculum Content Map

The teachers in this district wanted quick overview information about the sequence of units in five focus areas of the K–8 science curriculum. Such vertical information is easily available with the help of the computer. (1 page)

Map H: Secondary Mathematics Curriculum Map

Rather than simply listing the mathematics curriculum in terms of major areas for work, this map provides teachers with an overview through the course of a school year, September through June. Not only does this assist teachers as they look at past, present, and future experiences of their students, but it also provides opportunities to share materials and planning with other disciplines. (2 pages)

Map I: Cartographer Samples

These pages give a visual picture of the types of formats possible using a software program specifically designed to assist the mapping process. (4 pages)

Map J: Cartographer Browser—Elementary Example

This map is from a K–3 grade school. It shows the type of condensed and useful information that is possible on a school map. The teachers are in the throes of working on assessments and have yet to enter this on their maps. With a relatively clear sense of content and skills, that task should be easier. (3 pages)

Maps K1 through K5: Editing for Essential Questions—A Set of Elementary Maps

These maps underscore the value of returning to the initial raw data on the content entries and revising them to include essential questions. There is often genuine concern about the "coverage" of content rather than the "discover-age" of content. With careful editing through the use of essential questions, this concern is addressed. (5 pages)

Map L: Software Titles for Curriculum Integration

The media specialist now has the central role of assisting teachers with the grade-level selection of software and online services that will naturally link with curriculum. Working from the school maps, two media specialists put together a listing with questions, software titles, and vendors. The teams were attending a district workshop, hence, the reasons for the lack of grade level sequence. The media specialist basically sat with the maps and with the teams and compiled this list. (4 pages)

Map M: Software Purchases '95—Sorted

This shows how media specialists normally have a list of new purchases. Unless that list is tied to the curriculum map, it is unlikely to be used. (2 pages)

Maps N–Q

The set of maps displayed reflects the work of a suburban school district that has worked intensively over a year's time to collect content, skills, and assessment data. Of particular interest is the fact that teachers have revisited the maps to add detail and specificity to the data. There are interesting differences among the types of content reported at the elementary, middle, and high schools levels. Note the nature of the seminar titles for the middle school content section. There is general consistency in the skill section, where each entry begins with a verb—thus underscoring the process involved.

The teachers in this district are now reviewing the assessment portion of the maps by matching them with state standards. They're also sitting with colleagues at regularly scheduled building meetings to improve the quality of the assessments by bringing student work samples and examining the flow of the maps regarding student pieces. Next year they hope to revise the content with essential questions. (7 pages)

✧ ✧ ✧

MAP A

KINDERGARTEN CURRICULUM MAP

INTEGRATED TOPICS	SEPTEMBER	OCTOBER	NOVEMBER	DECEMBER	JANUARY	FEBRUARY	MARCH	APRIL	MAY	JUNE
Opening Meeting/Group Dismissal	← About Me ---	--- →	(Crossties Finger Plays School Search	- i.e., Grand Poetry	Central) - Counting	- Daily - Alphabet	Planning - Dressing Joke-Telling	- Calendar - Choral Unit	Weather Speaking	----- ↑
Language Arts/Reading Readiness	← ← ← Visual ← Following ← -- Autumn:	---- Same Discrim. Directions "W" Leaves -	Holiday, Different, - Visual - Left Questions - Poetry ----	Alphabet - Sequencing, Imagery To Right Experience ---- Winter.	Rhymes - Dot-to-Dot, - Letter Progression Charts, Stories Snow ------	Fine Motor - Listening Recognition - Top-Bottom - Scribble	Opposites - Comprehension - Appreciation Progression - Writing ---- Spring:	Classification Beginning of Literature Answering ---- Beginnings ----	Sounds --	↑ ↑ ↑ ↑ ↑
Math/Number Readiness	← ← ← ←	Counting/	Recognition Unifix Geo- Shapes	#'s 0 - 10 ---- → Cubes, Pattern Boards - Sorting	← Blocks, Problem Patterning	Counting/ Ordinal #'s Solving Sheets Sequencing	Recognition #'s - Colors Dot-to-Dot	0 - 100		↑ ↑ ↑
Gametime/Music/ Rhythms/Physical Activities	← ← ← ←		- Games - Fitness -	Individual Dramatization Rhythm	Skills - - Gross Melody - Winter Games	Instruments Motor Skills Movement				↑ ↑ ↑ ↑
Science/Social Studies/Health & Safety	---- Fall	Fire Topics---- Textures	Prevention Nutrition--- - Map Skills -	← Winter Safety - Environmental Family - ---- Tri-Town	Topics--- → Temperature - Awareness - Community (---- Health	← Spring Weather - Drug Program Helpers HLAY Curriculum ---	Topics --- → Sizes - - Body Parts 2000, Units 1 - 7	← Seeds → - Weights ---	Summer	Topics →
Skill/Centers Activity Time/Art	← ← ←	-Blocks- Listening ----Chalk	Housekeeping Station - Boards -	- Computer Manipulatives Fine Motor -	- Clay/ Play - Puzzles VCR	Dough - - Art Media (related)	Seasonal - Library -- videos)	Interest	Centers	↑ ↑ ↑

MAP B

5TH GRADE MATHEMATICS CURRICULUM MAP

Chattanooga School for the Liberal Arts   School Year: 1996–1997   Sample of Domain Map

ORGANIZING CONCEPTS	CHOICES	CHOICES	CHANGES	CHANGES	INTERDEPENDENCE	INTERDEPENDENCE	DIVERSITY	DIVERSITY	DIVERSITY
MONTHS	AUGUST/SEPTEMBER	OCTOBER	NOVEMBER	DECEMBER	JANUARY	FEBRUARY	MARCH	APRIL	MAY/JUNE
Related Literature									
Seminar Selections									
Field Studies									
Numeration/Number Theory	Value of numbers. Place value thru billions. Recognize: Standard form, word, name, prime/composite Expanded form – review Comparing/ordering billions	Decimals: Identify to 1000s – rounding off decimals comparing/ordering							
Operations/Computation	Mean/Average (review) Exponents: Scientific notation Factor Tree (intro)	Adding–subtracting–multiplying–dividing decimals to 1000s MASTERED		Fractions: Review lowest term– comparing/ordering. Multiples LCM– mixed numerals– changing improper/mixed. Add and subtract above. MASTERED	Fractions: renaming before subtraction – changing fractions to decimals. Decimals to fractions. MASTERED	Fractions: Multi-fractions By whole number By mixed number	Intro: Reciprocals – Dividing fractions By whole numbers By mixed numbers		Intro: Ration and Percent

MAP B, continued

5TH GRADE MATHEMATICS CURRICULUM MAP

Chattanooga School for the Liberal Arts   School Year: 1996—1997   Sample of Domain Map

ORGANIZING CONCEPTS	CHOICES	CHOICES	CHANGES	CHANGES	INTERDEPENDENCE	INTERDEPENDENCE	DIVERSITY	DIVERSITY	DIVERSITY
MONTHS	AUGUST/SEPTEMBER	OCTOBER	NOVEMBER	DECEMBER	JANUARY	FEBRUARY	MARCH	APRIL	MAY/JUNE
Measurements	Addition, multiplication, subtraction, division of whole numbers. MASTERED		Metric measure: conversion to other metric units. Measure to nearest millimeter. Measure weight or mass. Read temperature related units.	Liquid measurement: ozs., etc. Standard measurement: fractional parts of an inch. Area of rectangle: by formula					
Geometry								Recognize complex shapes: Guadra Latenia Polygons: review Congruency Intro: Measure angles using protractor.	Measure circle: radius and diameter
Problem Solving	Word problems dealing with above concepts.								Review time/money word problems.
Data Analysis		GRAPHING: reading	Continue graphing using measure knowledge.						
Graphs and Tables		Constructing tables/ charts – circle graph, line graph, bar graph, pictograph							
Number Sentences and Patterns									Ordered Pairs – Constructing and plotting points on graph.

MAP C

5TH GRADE INTEGRATED CURRICULUM MAP

Chattanooga School for the Liberal Arts   School Year: 1996—1997

ORGANIZING CONCEPTS	NEW BEGINNINGS ----	------------→	--------→	BALANCE----------	---------→	EXPANSION -----	---------→	INTERDEPENDENCE	------------→
MONTHS	AUGUST/SEPTEMBER	OCTOBER	NOVEMBER	DECEMBER	JANUARY	FEBRUARY	MARCH	APRIL	MAY/JUNE
Related Literature	The Talking Earth	Author Study	Witch of Blackbird Pond ------	-------------→		Caddie Woodlawn	Hatchet???	Lit Set on Various Cultures--------	-----------→ Independent Reading
Seminar Selections									
Field Studies	Sequoyah-Energy Connections		Williamsburg Jamestown	Nutcracker Ballet		Channel 3 TV Station		D.A.R.E. Picnic	
Forum/Current Events	Focus on people and countries making new beginnings			Focus on our struggle for independence		Focus on immigration effects on our country	Focus on government regulation and its effects on citizens	Focus on USA events and how we live together as a nation	Focus on exploration in various fields (medicine, law, etc.)
Social Studies	5 themes of Geography Explorers Native Americans	Colonization ----	-------------→	Declaration of Independence Bill of Rights and Constitution Branches of Government	Exploration Westward Expansion	Immigration to Ellis Island		USA supply geography states and capitals	Interdependence of North Am. Countries Interdependence of regions
Science	Energy: -------- Radiant/Geothermal Fossil Fuels/Nuclear Uses/Problems/ Sources Forms - Kinetic/Potential	-------------→	Machines & ------ Motion-Newton's Laws of Motion 6 Simple Machines Friction/Force	-------------→	Microbiology Observation Skills Microscope Skills Comparing Plant and Animal Cells	Plants/Ecosystems/ Biomes/Genetics Biome Study Wetlands Study Gregor Mendel – Heredity Tree/Flower Observations	Composting and Recycling -------------→ Environmental Conservation	Spring Garden	Human Body Wellness/Nutrition/ Physical Fitness Harvest Spring Garden Wellness Fair
Math	Place Value Mean/Average Exponents Computation Problems Solving	Decimals- to 100ths computation in all operations Graphing Problem Solving	Metric measure Continue Graphic Problem Solving	Standard Measure Fractions Problem Solving	Fractions Problem Solving	Fractions Problem Solving	Fractions Problem Solving	Reciprocals Divide fractions Problem Solving	Geometry complex shapes angles Problem Solving

MAP C, continued

5TH GRADE INTEGRATED CURRICULUM MAP

Chattanooga School for the Liberal Arts School Year: 1996–1997

ORGANIZING CONCEPTS	NEW BEGINNINGS ----→		BALANCE --------→			EXPANSION --------→		INTERDEPENDENCE --→	
MONTHS	AUGUST/SEPTEMBER	OCTOBER	NOVEMBER	DECEMBER	JANUARY	FEBRUARY	MARCH	APRIL	MAY/JUNE
Language Arts	Writing process Sentence study Writing workshop	Paragraph Study	Story writing Genre study both reading & writing	Parts of Speech		Figurative language Antonyms & synonyms	Conflict/solution Comparisons	Poems & stories from our 50 states	Publication of books and portfolios
Music	Focus on European— and Asian musical heritage brought to U.S. 1800–1900	----------→	----------→	Patriotic Music "Star Spangled Banner" origin Ives variations "America" Song collection		American Work Songs Railroad Cowboy Sailing	Mining Farming Slave	American composers Aaron Copland Charles Ives	
Art	European Influences- on American Art Presidential portraits Artist Copley	----------→ National Museum Slides	Duck Stamp National Contest	Photography Ellis Island Statue of Liberty	Color Theory	Afro-American Artist Remington, Catlin Westward Movement	Brandywine artist, New England	Andrew Wyeth	
Foreign Language									
Physical Education									
Learning/Behavior Skills	Learning modality and right/left brain Myself as learner	Team attitude	Listening	Note Taking	Cooperation	Problem----------- Solving-----------	----------→	Compromising	Communication----→
Technology	Math Skill games Reference support via varied CD-Rom such as: 500 Nations Encarta Atlas Art Gallery	Decimal Practice -----------	Metric conversion practice ----------- Division review	History Timeline game ----------- Climate & Weather manipulation exercises Spelling compre- hension	Critical thinking exercises ----------- Fraction +/-games -----------	Antonyms/Synonyms game Prefix/Suffix review Problem solving	----------- ----------- -----------	Fraction operations ----------→ ----------→ Keyboarding Skills ----------→ Maps & Atlas uses ----------→	
Assessments									

MAP D

8TH GRADE HUMANITIES TEAM

INTEGRATED TOPICS	SEPTEMBER	OCTOBER	NOVEMBER	DECEMBER	JANUARY	FEBRUARY	MARCH	APRIL	MAY	JUNE
Social Studies	Civil War	Reconstruction	Industrialization	Imperialism	World War I	Roaring '20s	New Deal '30s	WWII	'50s	'60s
English	Lincoln's Uncle Tom's PBS Civil Vocabulary---- Grammar---- Journal---- Free Reading----	Letters Cabins War Series	Black Boy Quarter Test Poetry Unit: Walt Whitman	The Robber Barons Inherit The Wind	For Whom The Bell Tolls	The Great Gatsby Quarter Test		Diary of Anne Frank Schindler's List	The Crucible	To Kill A Mockingbird
Social Studies	Point-of-View	Primary source: • photos • cause and effect • analysis	Debating Skills Mapping		Take a Stand Mapping		Identification Seeds of Conflict Analyzing Power			
English		Point-of-View • author's intent • conflict	Oral Presentation Editing Skills---		Free Verse Composition of Poetry		Note Taking Character Analysis	Settings in Stories	Play Analysis	
Social Studies	Civil War Anthology	TEST		Debate Contest	Persuasive Essay Debate and Arguments		-Maps and Analysis -Position Paper	Photo Essay	Graphic Organizer	Due: 3-D Time line of decades
English	Civil War Anthology	Descriptive Paragraphs	Portfolio Check		Poetry Analysis	Portfolio Check	Poetry Collection	Persuasive Essay	Role Play Commentary	FINAL

MAP E

9TH GRADE INTERDISCIPLINARY "LIFE SCIENCES" PROGRAM MAP

SUBJECT THEMES	QUARTER 1: TRUST	QUARTER 2: COMMUNICATION	QUARTER 3: TOLERANCE	QUARTER 4: RESPONSIBILITY
Health 9	Drug Education (Physiology & Prevention)	Family Living (Role models, sex, birth control, AIDS prevention)	Drug Education (Physiology & Prevention)	Family Living (Role models, sex, birth control, AIDS prevention)
Biology 9	Characteristics of Life (cells, biochemistry, metabolism)	Continuity of Life (reproduction & genetics)	Homeostasis (anatomy & physiology)	Patterns of Organization (evolution, ecology, & environment)
PA/Fitness	Cardiovascular Fitness (muscular strength & endurance)	Project Adventure (problem-solving skills)	Cardiovascular Fitness (muscular strength & endurance)	Project Adventure (problem-solving skills)

MAP F

11TH GRADE SCIENCE MAP

	SEPTEMBER	OCTOBER	NOVEMBER	DECEMBER	JANUARY	FEBRUARY	MARCH	APRIL	MAY	JUNE
	Matter	Symbols Equations	Molecular Structure	Periodic Table	Bonds Atoms Molecules	Gas Laws	Solids Liquids Solutions	Acids Salts	Kinetics Equilibrium	Review
	Observation Lab Writing	Computer • CD Rom use • Graphic • Organizers	Model Formations	Essay Writing	Historical	Empirical Research Skills Observations / Speaking	Skills	Posing	Problem	
	Notebooks------ Lab Reports ------ Lab Performance--	Data-sheets	3-D Model report / Quarter Test	-Multiple choice -Essay	Chart with Findings / Quarter Test	3-D Model / Research Study - / Analytic Essay	Chart with Findings ------	Position Paper / Quarter Test		FINAL

MAP G

K-8 SCIENCE CURRICULUM CONTENT MAP

TOPICS	KINDERGARTEN	1ST GRADE	2ND GRADE	3RD GRADE	4TH GRADE	5TH GRADE	6TH GRADE	7TH GRADE	8TH GRADE
Environment	Seasons	Seasonal Changes Weather	Ecology Seashore		Water Cycle Geography	Ecosystems Field Forest Marsh Pond Meteorology	Outdoor Ed Saltmarsh	Outdoor Studies Microbiology Immunology Genetics Environmental Issues Biomes Botany	Chemical vs. Physical Changes Heat and Temperature
Physical World	Sink & Float	Heavy & Light Attributes Magnets	States of Matter	Buoyancy	Electricity Light Sound		Matter Physical & Chemical Properties	Chemical Symbols & Formulas	Reaction Rates Newton's Law of Motion Light Atomic Theory And Structure
Human Body	General Awareness	Nutrition Five Senses	Nutrition	Safety	Drug Awareness	Respiratory Parts & Care	Circulatory Drug & Alcohol Awareness	Viruses, Diseases, AIDS	Mental Health
Living Things		Living vs. Nonliving	Plant Cycles	Animal Life Cycles Crayfish	Animals Habitats Adaptation Plants Pollination		Living Things Plant & Animal Cells Voyage of the Mimi II	Scientific Skills: The microscope Cell structure & function	Organic Chemistry
Earth and Space			Solar System	How Things Work Together		Solar System Astronomy	Changes in the Earth's Crust	Osmosis & Diffusion	Forces Spectra Analysis

MAP H

SECONDARY MATHEMATICS CURRICULUM MAP

GRADE LEVEL	SEPTEMBER	OCTOBER	NOVEMBER	DECEMBER	JANUARY	FEBRUARY	MARCH	APRIL	MAY	JUNE
Grade 6	Add & Sub Whole Numbers Place value, ordering, Rounding, Exponents S-estimation, map reading	Mult. & Div. Whole Numbers Memorize Times Tables Guess & Check, Averaging	Graphing Points, Tables, Coordinate Geom, Decimals— ordering, compare patterns, write equations	Decimals-Mult & Div Problem Solving-multistep S-Short cuts in Div.	Number Theory - GCF, LCM, Primes, Factorization, Fractions - Lowest terms, Mixed, problem solving	Multiplying fractions, division, reciprocals, meas-urement/geometry, perimeter, area, volume	ratio, proportion, similar tri. & rect., probability, percents, proportions to solve	Voyage of the Mimi Interdisciplinary unit, geometry - definitions, lines, parallel and perpend.	Geom—polygons, congruency, circle parts, solids, pi, symmetry/ reflections patterns, transformations	Integers - add & subtract Coordinate axes - 4 quad Metric system, labs
Grade 7	Whole Numbers, Properties, S-Computation, Rounding Exponents, Estimation	Expressions, Equations, Decimals, Place Value, S-Solving, Evaluating	Statistics & Probability S-Interpreting Graphs S-Environmental Uses	Number Theory Greatest Common Factor Least Common Multiple	Fractions, S-comparing, computation	Fractions, ratio & proportion, S-conversion, solving	Percents, S-Conversion, S-Sales Tax, Discounts	Geometry-polygons, circles, area, volume, circum., Measurement: Metric & U.S.	Crime Unit Statistics, Percent Graphs in daily life	Integers - add & subtract, multiply and divide, S-meaning, computation
Grade 8	Set Notation, Theory, Problem Solving, Order of Operations, S-Approaches to Solving	Variable Expression, Formulas, Intro to Equation Solving, S-Combining Like Terms	Intro to Inequalities Customary Measurement Decimal Concepts S-Operations on Decimals	Decimal Concepts Roman Numerals Integers S-applying decimals	Integers – Mult., Div., Equations, variable exp. Negative exponents, Scientific notation	Fractions, GCF, LCM, expressions and equations, S-computation, and evaluating	Ratio, Proportion, percent, S-Cross products, S-frac-Dec.-% equivalents	Percent Applications, Energy unit-interpret graphs, percent and info S-real life applications	Percent applications Cartesian Coordinates Geometry-Identify shapes S-Geometry Vocabulary	Geometry, Perimeter, area, volume, review S-Recall, organize material
Course I (9, 10, 11, 12)	Introduction to Algebra Domain, Range Solve ax+b=c	Introduction to Symbolic Logic and Truth Tables	Arithmetic of Polynomials	Solving Complex Linear Questions and Inequalities	Introducion to geometry Terminology Transformations	Factoring Polynomials	Arithmetic of algebraic factions Intro to Probability	Graphing linear equations & inequalities Intro to statistics	Solving systems of equations & inequalities Intro to radicals	Review
Course II (9, 10, 11)	Symbolic Logic S-Proofs S-Validity of Arguments	Geometric Proofs Postulates, Definitions, Theorems, S-Inductive vs. Deductive	Triangle Congruence and Inequalities, S-Solve eq and ineq S-compare properties	Perpendicular and Parallel lines - Angle Sums - Polygons and Angles	Quadrilaterals Irrational Numbers	Ratio & proportion Similarity Right Tri. Trig. S-Recognize Sim. Shapes	Coordinate Graphs Quadratic Equation S-apply formulas to figures on graph	Quadratic equation, Locus, S-apply quad eq. to geom S-Solve simultaneous eq.	Transformation geom. Probability, algebraic fractions S-use permutations & comb.	Algebraic fractions Review

MAP H, continued

SECONDARY MATHEMATICS CURRICULUM MAP

GRADE LEVEL	SEPTEMBER	OCTOBER	NOVEMBER	DECEMBER	JANUARY	FEBRUARY	MARCH	APRIL	MAY	JUNE
Course III (10, 11, 12)	Group Field Properties Arithmetic of Rational Algebraic Fractions	Geometry of the Circle Arithmetic of Irrational Numbers	Functions Transformations Conic Sections	Intro to Trig Functions	Graphing Trig Functions and Exponential Functions	Logarithmic Functions	Proving Trig Identities Solving Trig Equations	Algebra in complex number field	Probability & statistics	Review
Intro to Course I (9, 10)	Linear Equations Combine Like Terms Word Problems S–add, sub, mult, div	Substitution (formulas) Two step Linear Equations, Word Problems, S–estimating	Exponents Factoring (Prime) Order of Operations S–Raise to power, GCF	Linear Eq. Variables both sides – Inequalities Linear Graphs, Word Problems	Multistep Inequalities Coordinate axes Reading graphs S–plot points	Graph linear equations, slope, solve graphically & ck, S–Draw graph, substitute	Graph Inequalities, ratio, proportion, % Word problems, S–cross mult	Similar triangles, geometry – shapes & properties, perimeter, area, coord. Geom. S–Proportion, shapes	Mean, Median, Mode Probability, Symbolic Logic, S–add count	Truth Tables Review for RCT
Topics in II (10, 11, 12)	Language of Geometry Angles S–Measure & Recognize S–Construction	Polygons & Plyhedra S–Recognize Figures Convex vs Concave triangles, quads	Transformations Triangles & Inequalities S–Use symmetry S–Medians, Altitudes	Parallel Lines Transversals & angles Triangle & poly angles	Quadrilaterals, S–Recognize and find parts	Perimeter an darea tri, quad, circle, similarity, S–Calc. & use formulas	Similarity, Square roots & rt. tri., S–Pythagorean Th., S–Special Rt. Triangles	Circles – central angles, inscribed angles, S–measure angles & arcs	Coordinate graphs, distance, midpoint, S–use formulas, S–graph types	Coordinate graphs, slpe, eq. Of circle, review
Topics in III (11, 12)	Polynomial Operations Rational Expressions Factoring S–Operations on fractions	Geometry of Circle Arcs, Angles, Chords, Secants, Tangents, S–Recognize Parts	Irrational Numbers Quadratic Formula Radical Equations S–operations on radicals	Transformations Coordinate Plane S–plotting & interpreting	Statistics, Normal curve, Standard deviation, S–practical application	Probability, Binomial Theorem, S–practical applications	Trigonometry, Unit Circle, Sine, Cosine, Tangent, S–recognize basic trig	Relations & functions, Exponential functions, Domain and range	Complex numbers Quadratic Equations/w complex roots S–intro to imaginary #'s	Law of sines, law of cosines, review
Pre Calculus (11, 12)	Mathematical Induction Quadratic & Absolute Value Inequalities	Relations & Functions Complex Numbers De Moivres Theorem	Polar Coordinate Graphs Sequences and Series Neighborhoods & limits	Continuity Functions (Polynomial, Piece-Wise, Rational)	Intro to derivative Synthetic substitution Factor and remainder th.	Max, min, pt of inflection, polynomial sketching, polynomial equations	radical functions, max-min word problems, conic sections	conic sections matrices 7 determinants matrix operations	Matrices-solve equations Rules for finding F'(x) Velocity & acceleration	Integration for area Review
AP Calculus (12)	Functions, Domain, Range, Limits, and Graphs Slope of curve S–Factore, Solve & check	Rules for derivatives Implicit Differentiation Eq. Of Tangent & Normal S–Graph, solve & check	Inverse Functions & der, Trig functions & der. Chain rule, continuity related rates	Mean value theorem, L'Hopitals Rule, area – limit of rect.- sum S–Domain & Range	Definite Integral Integral applications Area under curve, distance velocity, acceol, volume	Exponential functions, Natural log function, derivative and applic. Of expo and log functions	Special trig integration, integration by parts, area by trapezoidal approx	Special case – problems review for AP	Review for AP, Practice exams	Integration – partialfraction series and sequences

MAP I

CARTOGRAPHER BROWSER—SEMESTER 1 HORIZONTAL

	SEPTEMBER	OCTOBER	NOVEMBER	DECEMBER	JANUARY
KINDERGARTEN TEAM	Content: Introduction to School: 1. Meet the teacher 2. Meet classmates 3. Tour the classroom 4. Introduce centers 5. Tour the school 6. Meet school personel 7. Bus and traffic rules 8. School and classroom rules Graph how you get to school Skills: Assessment:	Content: Study of "Me" Class trips: 1. Conclin's Orchards 2. Van Riper's Farm Puppet Show - Mind Your Manners Study of Christopher Columbus Halloween Fire Safety Classroom Responsibility: 1. Jobs 2. Homework 3. Must do's 4. Can do's Skills: Assessment:	Content: Holidays: 1. Election Day 2. Veteran's Day 3. Thanksgiving Feast, discussed being thankful, and how Indians helped the Pilgrims. The Great Body Shop - 1. To cite reasons for rules and to recognize authority figures. 2. Play song "15 ways to stay out of trouble." 3. Safety when crossing street, seatbelt, bike and fire safety. Study of Me - 1. Family Skills: Assessment	Content: Study of Me - 1. What I like to do best 2. Houses 3. Pets 4. What I would like to learn about Holidays: 1. Hanukkah 2. Christmas Skills: Assessment:	Content: Study of Me: 1. Favorite clothes, t.v. show, person and game. 2. What I like to do with my hands Holidays: 1. Martin Luther King Jr. 2. Rights and equality The Great Body Shop: 1. My Body is special Skills: Assessment:
SOCIAL STUDIES					

MAP I, continued

CARTOGRAPHER BROWSER—SEMESTER 1 HORIZONTAL

	SEPTEMBER	OCTOBER	NOVEMBER	DECEMBER	JANUARY
1ST GRADE TEAM	**Content:** Rules: class rules, teamwork, cooperation, Johnny Appleseed, Labor Day, self-esteem, self-respect **Skills:** To gather and use information, to listen to others, to accept responsibility as a group member, to explore the United States frontier, to integrate science skills, to recognize connection of food cycle and weather, to present an awareness of our national heritage, to respect others as well as ourselves **Assessment:**	**Content:** Columbus Day, maps, world exploration, risk taking, Halloween, Fire Prevention Week, safety, self-esteem, self-respect **Skills:** To gather and use information, to listen to others, to accept responsibility as a group member, to explore United States history, to recognize and practice safety skills, to be aware and know how and when to use 911 emergency system, to respect others as well as ourselves, to become aware of location and direction on a map or globe, to develop an awareness of the physical shape and boundaries of the United States/world **Assessment:**	**Content:** Veterans' Day, Election Day, how our political structure, voting, citizenship, Thanksgiving, family, history/heritage, traditions, self-esteem, self-respect **Skills:** To gather and use information, to listen to others, to accept responsibility as a group member, to explore United States history, to respect others as well as ourselves, to become aware of location and direction on a map or globe, to develop an awareness of the physical shape and boundaries of the United States/world, to appreciate family values, heritage and customs, to recognize that we elect our leaders, to develop an understanding and respect for our past **Assessment:**	**Content:** Christmas, Hanukkah, families, cultural diversities, traditions around the world, self-esteem, self-respect **Skills:** To gather and use information, to listen to others, to accept responsibility as a group member, to respect others as well as ourselves, to become aware of location and direction on a map or globe, to appreciate family values, heritage and customs, to develop an appreciation of different/similar values, attitudes, beliefs, and behaviors **Assessment:**	**Content:** New Year celebration, Martin Luther King Jr., cultural diversity, civil rights, peaceful changes, laws, fairness, self-esteem, self-respect **Skills:** To gather and use information, to listen to others, to accept responsibility as a group member, to develop an appreciation for interaction with others in decision making, to respect others as well as ourselves, to become aware of location and direction on a map or globe, to appreciate family values, heritage and customs, k to develop an appreciation of different/similar values, attitudes, beliefs and behaviors, to develop an understanding that change is sometimes necessary for rules to be effective and relevant **Assessment:**
SOCIAL STUDIES FIRST					

MAP I, continued

CARTOGRAPHER BROWSER—SEMESTER 1 HORIZONTAL

	SEPTEMBER	OCTOBER	NOVEMBER	DECEMBER	JANUARY
2ND GRADE TEAM	**Content:** School and Class Rules Maps and Globe **Skills:** School and Class Rules – appropriate behavior, school and class situations Maps and globe -- identify terms, maps, globe, directions, landforms, continents, oceans, north and south poles, equator Assessment	**Content:** Fire prevention Different types of groups **Skills:** Fire Prevention: Safety, stop, drop, and roll, E.D.I.T.H., 911, how to exit, fire safety in the home Different types of groups – family, school, extended family, clubs, teams, friends, interests, hobbies, sports Assessment	**Content:** Holidays around the world **Skills:** Holidays around the world – specific holiday customs: food, clothing traditions, history Assessment	**Content:** Holidays around the world **Skills:** Holidays around the world – specific holiday customs: food, clothing traditions, history Assessment	**Content:** Communities Martin Luther King Jr. **Skills:** Communities – three types: rural, urban, suburban neighborhoods within a community, capital cities, facts about our country Martin Luther King Jr. – discuss life and relate to modern day times Assessment
SOCIAL STUDIES					

MAP I, continued

CARTOGRAPHER BROWSER—SEMESTER 1 HORIZONTAL

	SEPTEMBER	OCTOBER	NOVEMBER	DECEMBER	JANUARY
3RD GRADE TEAM	Content: Introduction of maps and globe skills Research skills introduced Interdisciplinary use of graphs and charts Skills: Assessment:	Content: Learning about maps and globes A globe is a model of the earth. A map shows where things are in relation to one another. A compass rose may be used to indicate directions on a map. Colors and symbols are used on a map. Maps are drawn for different purposes. A map scale indicates distance on a map. The rotation of earth causes night and day. Earth is divided into hemispheres. An atlas is a book of maps. Assessment:	Content: We all live in communities. Food, clothing, and shelter are basic needs. Communities help people meet their basic needs. Communities vary in size and location. There are 50 states in the U.S. Washington D.C. is the capital of the U.S. There are 7 continents and four oceans in the world. Every community has a history. A picture graph is one way to organize information. Assessment	Content: People Build Communities The Indians were the first people in North America. Colonists came from different countries to settle America. Colonies fought to become independent Pioneers moved west. Trading centers grew along railroads. Skills: Assessment	Content: Rural Communities Natural resources must be used wisely. Jobs depend on natural resources. Towns grew where natural resources were. Climate determines the type of crop. Land preserved for national parks. Environment must be protected from pollution. Rural communities exist all over world. Skills: Assessment:
SOCIAL STUDIES					

MAP J

CARTOGRAPHER BROWSER—SEMESTER 2 HORIZONTAL

	FEBRUARY	MARCH	APRIL	MAY	JUNE

KINDERGARTEN TEAM	Content:
	Holidays:
	1. Abraham Lincoln
	2. Valentine's Day
	3. George Washington
	
	The Great Body Shop:
	Continue My Body is Special
	Skills:
	Assessment:
		Content:
		The Great Body Shop:
		1. Health
		  a. Betsy brushes her teeth
		2. Star Mobile
		  a. Special aspects of yourself
		
		Holiday:
		1. St. Patrick's Day
		Skills:
		Assessment:
			Content:
			The Great Body Shop:
			1. Feelings
			2. Health-body clean and healthy
			3. Good and bad touches
			
			Transportation Unit:
			1. Land
			2. Sea
			3. Air
			Skills:
			Assessment:
				Content:
				Holidays:
				Mother's Day
				2. Memorial Day
				Multicultural Study: Hawaii
				1. Luau for LI week
				A. Legend
				B. Dance
				C. Song
				D. Costume
				F. Story
				G. Decorations and art/puppet
				
				The Great Body Shop:
				1. Drugs
				2. Community Helpers
				A. Dentist
				B. Doctor
				C. Police Officers
				D. Fire People
				Skills:
				Assessment:
					Content:
					Community Helpers: Summer Safety
					1. Teachers
					2. Nurses
					3. Librarians
					4. Truck Drivers
					5. Sales Personnel
					6. Butchers/Bakers
					7. Postal Workers
					
					Holidays:
					1. Father's Day
					2. Flag Day
					Skills:
					Assessment:

SOCIAL STUDIES					

MAP J, continued

CARTOGRAPHER BROWSER—SEMESTER 2 HORIZONTAL

	FEBRUARY	MARCH	APRIL	MAY	JUNE
1ST GRADE TEAM	**Content:** Groundhog Day, Chinese New Year, Lincoln's Birthday, Valentine's Day, Washington's Birthday, patriotic/national symbols, friendship, self-esteem, self-respect **Skills:** To gather and use information, to listen to others, to accept responsibility as a group member, to develop an appreciation for interaction with others in decisionmaking, to respect others as well as ourselves, to become aware of location and direction on a map or globe, to appreciate family values, heritage and customs, to develop an appreciation of different/similar values, attitudes, beliefs and behaviors, to develop an understanding that change is sometimes necessary for rules to be effective and relevant, to develop an appreciation and understanding of our leaders of the past, to develop an awareness that change is natural and will continue. **Assessment:**	**Content:** St. Patrick's Day, cultural diversity, community workers, family, self-esteem, self-respect **Skills:** To gather an duse information, to listen to others, to accept responsibility as a group member, to develop an appreciation for interaction with others in decision-making, to respect others as well as ourselves, to appreciate family values, heritage, and customs, to develop an appreciation of different/similar values, attitudes, beliefs and behaviors, to develop an awareness that change is natural and will continue into the future. **Assessment:**	**Content:** April fool's Day, Easter, Passover, self-esteem, self-respect **Skills:** To gather and use information to listen to others, to accept responsibility as a group member, to respect others as well as ourselves, to appreciate family values, heritage and customs, to develop an appreciation of different/similar values, attitudes, beliefs and behaviors, to rely on others to help meet our needs and wants. **Assessment:**	**Content:** self esteem, self respect, Memorial Day, patriotic symbols, maps, Mother's Day **Skills:** To gather and use information, to accept responsibility as a group member, to explore United States history, to respect others as well as ourselves, to appreciate family values, heritage and customs, to develop an understanding and respect for our past, to develop an understanding and appreciation for other's point of view. **Assessment:**	**Content:** self esteem, self respect, Flag Day, Independence Day, Father's Day **Skills:** To gather and use information, to accept responsibility as a group member, to develop an awareness of national heritage, to respect others as well as ourselves, to appreciate family values, heritage and customs, to develop an understanding and appreciation for others' points of view, to develop an awareness of one's attitude and responsibility toward our nation's symbols (flag) **Assessment**
SOCIAL STUDIES FIRST					

MAP J, *continued*

CARTOGRAPHER BROWSER—SEMESTER 2 HORIZONTAL

	FEBRUARY	MARCH	APRIL	MAY	JUNE
2ND GRADE TEAM / **SOCIAL STUDIES**	Content: George Washington/Abe Lincoln; China. Skills: Washington/Lincoln: Discussion of their life and relevance for today; China: holiday, country, people. Assessment:	Content: Earth Day. Skills: Earth Day - Environmental responsibility. Assessment:	Content: Current Events. Skills: Current Events - events as they happen throughout the year. Assessment:	Content: Resources. Skills: Resources - definition of terms, basic needs, goods, services, needs and wants, natural resources, energy, how paper is made, reduce, recycle, reuse. Assessment:	Content: Review of American History. Skills: Review of American History - famous landmarks, colonies, pioneers, presidents, songs, flags. Assessment:
3RD GRADE TEAM / **SOCIAL STUDIES**	Content: Urban Communities. Cities may be divided into different areas according to their primary use. People who work in the cities often live in suburban areas. The location of a city determines the types of industry and the kinds of goods manufactured there. Good transportation is important in all urban areas of the world. Skills: Assessment:	Content: Communities Change. Communities grow and change. People contribute to community growth. Inventions change structure of communities. People plan future of communities. Through history people learn about the community's past. Skills: Assessment:	Content: Communities need laws. Homes, schools, and communities need rules. Laws are made by leaders. Leaders are elected by community people. People and leaders find ways to solve community problems. Skills: Assessment:	Content: Washington, D.C. Study of U.S. capital. Study of capital history. Rights and responsibilities of citizens. Obeying laws and voting are responsibilities of citizens. Skills: Assessment:	

MAP K1

EDITING FOR ESSENTIAL QUESTIONS

Third Grade Literacy Map

SEPTEMBER	Family Album 1. What special activities do you share with your family? 2. What are the five story elements?
OCTOBER	Family Album 1. What is exaggeration? 2. What are examples of exaggeration?
NOVEMBER	Friendship 1. What is realistic fiction? 2. Why do characters in stories act the way they do?
DECEMBER	Friendship 1. Why are a character's actions important to the reader?
JANUARY	Mysteries of the Deep 1. What are the characteristics of nonfiction text? 2. What are some mysteries of the water?
FEBRUARY	Mysteries of the Deep 1. Why is it important in writing to include main ideas and supporting details?
MARCH	Beverly Cleary 1. What types of stories does Beverly Cleary write? 2. What do you know about Beverly Cleary?
APRIL	Beverly Cleary 1. Who are some of the characters in Beverly Cleary's books and what are they like?
MAY	Once Upon a Time 1. What are fairytales and/or folktales? 2. What are the elements of a fairy/folktale?
JUNE	Beware of Trouble 1. What is a fantasy? 2. What are the characteristics of fantasy adventure literature? (Dr. DeSoto) It's Magic 1. What are the characteristics of a biography? (Houdini)

MAP K2

EDITING FOR ESSENTIAL QUESTIONS

5th Grade Reading Map

SEPTEMBER	**Long Ago and Far Away** What are the characteristics of traditional folktales with regards to cultures of the world?
OCTOBER	How do we interpret theme and symbolism in a traditional folktale?
NOVEMBER	**Operation Wildlife** How do we identify main idea and supporting details in a narrative nonfiction story?
DECEMBER	How do we recognize characteristics of a narrative nonfiction?
JANUARY	**Solutions** How do we identify and map story elements, such as conflict, plot, and sequence of events in a fictional story?
FEBRUARY (1 week)	
FEBRUARY	**Danger Zone** What is the importance of rising action, climax, and falling action in a suspenseful story?
MARCH (2 weeks)	How does the author make a story suspenseful? How do we identify multiple cause–effect relationships in a suspenseful story?
MARCH	**To Be Continued** How do we use visualization to aid the understanding of characters and events in a fantasy story?
APRIL	How does an author use point of view in a fantasy story?
MAY	**Journey Into Space** How do we generate questions and answers about a nonfiction story regarding current space exploration?
JUNE	What are the uses of personal narratives?

MAP K3

5th Grade Science Curriculum Map

SEPTEMBER	**Activities of Green Plants** In what ways do plants perform life process of all living things? How do plants perform the process photosynthesis to make their own food?
OCTOBER	**Plant Growth and Response** In what ways do tropisms help plants to grow and react to their environments? How do plants adapt to different environmental conditions?
NOVEMBER	**Invertebrates** What are the characteristics of the different classes of invertebrates? How do the different classes of invertebrates perform the five life processes?
DECEMBER	**Vertebrates** What are the characteristics of the different classes of vertebrates? How do the different classes of vertebrates carry out the five life processes?
JANUARY **FEBRUARY**	**The Digestive System** What are the main organs of the digestive system and how do they function as a system? What happens to food as it moves through the mechanical and the chemical digestive system?
MARCH **APRIL**	**The Circulatory System** What are the main organs of the circulatory system, and how do they function as a system? How does blood move through the circulatory system? What are the components of the blood? What are the parts of the heart and how does blood move through it?
MAY	**The Respiratory System** What are the main organs of the respiratory system and how do they function as a system? What life-giving exchange takes place in the lungs? **The Nervous System** What are the organs of the nervous system and how do they function as a system? What are the main parts of the brain?
JUNE	**Human Growth and Development** What causes the onset of adolescence? What physical changes occur as a boy or girl goes through adolescence? What hygiene is necessary to keep an adolescent's body healthy during the adolescence period? How does a baby develop in a mother's uterus and how is a baby born? What care is required for a newborn baby? Review of body systems and preparation for final exam

MAP K4

EDITING FOR ESSENTIAL QUESTIONS

6th Grade Curriculum Map

SUBJECT	SOCIAL STUDIES	MATH
SEPTEMBER	**Earth's Geography:** How does the geography influence the climate of an area? How does geography of an environment influence the culture of an area?	Review whole numbers properties and place values/introduction to problem solving: How would we connect whole number properties and place value with everyday life? What purpose do key words serve in problem solving?
OCTOBER	**Early People:** How have early people developed unique ways of adapting to their environments to solve their basic needs?	**Decimals:** How do we use comparing, rounding, and estimating of decimals in everyday life?
NOVEMBER	**Ancient Egypt:** How did the ancient Egyptians make good use of their geographical environment? How has the study of archaeology helped us to understand ancient civilizations?	**Decimals:** How do we use comparing, rounding, and estimating of decimals in everyday life?
DECEMBER	**Four Early Civilizations:** How have the legacies in law and religion affected later civilizations?	**Graphing, Data, Statistics:** How can we display collected statistical data in a graphics visual manner? How do we apply range, mean, median, and mode to real world problems?
JANUARY	**Ancient Greece and Ancient Rome:** How did these civilizations spread the philosophy of democracy, art, religion, science, laws, and the study of philosophy into modern western civilizations?	**Fractions:** How can we use fractions in our world?
FEBRUARY	**Religion:** How did the religions of Judaism, Islam, and Christianity develop and how did they influence the development of civilizations?	**Fractions:** How can we use fractions in our world?
MARCH	**Middle Ages, Renaissance, Reformation:** How did the desire for knowledge help Europeans advance their civilizations? How did the Reformation bring about the changes in Europe?	**Ratio, Proportions, and Probability:** How are ratios, proportions, and probability used in real life situations?
APRIL	**Exploration:** How did the desire to explore and discover advance the early Europeans geographic and scientific knowledge? **Modern Nations:** How did revolutions and World Wars create a democratic west and a communist east?	**Percent:** How do percents relate to decimals and fractions?
MAY	**Modern Nations:** How did the collapse of Communism usher in a new era of democracy?	**Geometry and Measurement:** What are the various forms of measurement and how can they be applied in daily life?
JUNE	**Traditional Tales:** How is irony, exaggeration, and figurative language used in folk-tales?	**Geometry and Measurement:** How do I compute area and perimeter? What are some real-world applications?

MAP K5

EDITING FOR ESSENTIAL QUESTIONS

Math Curriculum Map

Month	Essential Questions
SEPTEMBER	Where are numbers found among us and how do they affect our daily lives? How does the estimation, rounding, comparing, and ordering of whole numbers and decimals aid in problem solving? How is a calculator used to find math patterns and verify sums and differences?
OCTOBER	How can writing algebraic formulas help us to solve problems with one variable? How do we use multiples and factors to find products and quotients of whole numbers?
NOVEMBER	How is mental math used to solve problems and check reasonableness of answers?
DECEMBER	How do we gather and organize data to aid in the problem solving process? What is the relationship between shapes and measurement?
JANUARY	How do we use decimal products and quotients to decide on a strategy to solve problems?
FEBRUARY	What is the relationship between decimals and fractions?
MARCH	What are the different ways fractions are used to represent parts of a whole?
APRIL	Why is it necessary to rename fractions and mixed numbers to solve problems with sums and differences? When do we use a fraction of a fraction in everyday life? (Fractional products and quotients)
MAY	What is the relationship between fractions and percents? Where are percents found in the world around us?
JUNE	How is probability used to predict outcome in problem solving? What are the relationships between surface area perimeter and volume in regular and irregular shapes?

MAP L

SOFTWARE TITLES FOR CURRICULUM INTEGRATION

TOPIC	GRADE	QUESTIONS	SOFTWARE TITLES	VENDOR
AFRICAN CULTURES	9	How does geography influence the culture? Imperialism	CD Encyclopedia Africa Trail PC Globe World GeoGraph Slide show (KidPix or Claris Works) Word processing, database, spreadsheet	MECC (Mac, Win) Broderbund MECC (Mac) Broderbund Claris
BEGINNING CIVILIZATIONS WESTERN HEMISPHERE	5	Aztecs, Mayans Mound builders, Woodlands	Amazon Trail Maya Quest North American Indians	MECC (Mac, DOS, Win) MECC (Mac, Win) Quanta
COMING OF AGE	9	Romeo & Juliet roles of choice and fate	Decisions, Decisions Series Choosing Success Time, Life & Works of Shakespeare	Tom Snyder CCC
CYCLES	3	Life Cycles, spiders farming, rural/urban time, patterns in math the number 8 Charlotte's Web	Opening Night Math Keys	MECC (Mac, Win) MECC (Mac, Win)
GIFTS OF ANCIENT GREEKS	6	Influences Legacy of gifts	CD Encyclopedia PC Globe Total History World GeoGraph Ancient Lands Exploring Ancient Cities Spreadsheets Use internet access	Broderbund Bureau Elect. Publ. MECC (Mac) Microsoft Sumeria

MAP L, continued

SOFTWARE TITLES FOR CURRICULUM INTEGRATION

TOPIC	GRADE	QUESTIONS	SOFTWARE TITLES	VENDOR
HEALTHY ADOLESCENTS	7	What does it mean to be a healthy adolescent? Human Body Systems Health-related issues for an adolescent	Decisions, Decisions: Drinking & Driving Decisions, Decisions: AIDS Decisions, Decisions: Substance Abuse A.D.A.M. BodyScope How Your Body Works Use internet access	Tom Snyder Tom Snyder Tom Snyder Broderbund MECC (Mac) Mindscape
HUMAN INTERACTIONS WITH NATURAL RSOURCES	6	How does what we do to our environment affect our future? What influences our use of resources?	Oregon Trail Decisions, Decisions: The Environment Decisions, Decisions: Urbanization Time Liner	MECC (Mac, DOS, Win) Tom Snyder Tom Snyder Tom Snyder
IMMIGRANTS	3	Multicultural society Dolls/family trees Thanksgiving Molly's Pilgrim	History Makers Apple Works Immigration	MECC (Apple II) Apple Works
LIFE AFTER DEATH IN ANCIENT EGYPT	6	Pharaohs & Pyramids	CD Encyclopedia PC Globe Total History World GeoGraph Ancient Lands Exploring Ancient Cities Spreadsheets	Broderbund Bureau Elect. Publ. MECC (Mac) Microsoft Sumeria
NATIVE AMERICAN CULTURE	4	Art/Storytelling	CD Encyclopedia Oneida Nation home page KidPix	Internet Broderbund

MAP L, continued

SOFTWARE TITLES FOR CURRICULUM INTEGRATION

TOPIC	GRADE	QUESTIONS	SOFTWARE TITLES	VENDOR
NATIVE AMERICAN INFLUENCE	4	Who were Native Americans? Who were early colonists? How did the two cultures get along?	CD Encyclopedia Oneida Nation home page	Internet
PATTERNS, PATTERNS EVERYWHERE	K-1	Patterns around us	TessemMania Math Keys KidPix Tabletop Junior Math Sammy's Science House	MECC (Mac, Win) MECC (Mac, Win) Broderbund Broderbund Edmark
PEOPLE IN EUROPE DURING WWII	6	Causes & effects importance of geography technology – solved some problems, caused new ones	CD Encyclopedia Decisions, Decisions Milestones of 20th Century Point of View World's Greatest Speeches CNN Time Capsule Time Almanac Explorapedia	Tom Snyder Scholastic Scholastic Compact Publishing Microsoft
PILGRIMS: PROBLEM SOLVING	1	Cooperation, interdependence Problems on homeland & with voyage Food, shelter, interaction with Native Americans	KidPix Explorapedia	Broderbund Microsoft
PLANTS	K-2	Why are plants important to my life? What are plants and how do they grow? How do plants adapt to their environment?	Explorapedia KidPix Wooly's Garden Secrets of Nature	Microsoft Broderbund MECC (Apple II) Smart Works
PRESIDENT OF THE U.S.	5	What does the president do? What is required to run? How is the president chosen? What are the problems with the way we elect a president?	Presidents CD Origins of the Constitution Presidential Inquiry The Campaign Trail	Queue MECC (Mac) Tom Snyder

MAP L, continued

SOFTWARE TITLES FOR CURRICULUM INTEGRATION

TOPIC	GRADE	QUESTIONS	SOFTWARE TITLES	VENDOR
QUALIFY OF LIFE IN TECHNOLOGICAL WORLD	12	Endangered species National parks Toxic waste	CD Encyclopedia History in Motion CNN Time Capsule Time Almanac Word processing, database, spreadsheet Use Internet access	Scholastic
STRUCTURES	10	Social Studies – Biology parallels	Claris Works slide show KidPix A.D.A.M. CNN Time Capsule	Claris Broderbund Broderbund
SURVIVAL	5	Adaptation, evolution, immigration, genetic engineering	CD Encyclopedia Exploradpedia	Microsoft
WORKING THROUGH CONFLICT	2	Why do I want to get along with other students? What can I do to get along with other students? How can we share what we've learned with other students?	Storybook Weaver Choices, Choices: On the Playground Choices, Choices: Taking Responsibility	MECC (Mac, DOS, Win) Tom Snyder Tom Snyder
WORLD WAR II	6	Key People Worldwide conditions Consequences for nations Effect on world politics	CD Encyclopedia Decisions, Decisions Milestones of 20th Century Point of View World's Greatest Speeches CNN Time Capsule Time Almanac Explorapedia Word processing, database, spreadsheet	Tom Snyder Scholastic Scholastic Microsoft

MAP M

SOFTWARE PURCHASES '95—SORTED

CD-ROM TITLE	TYPE	PUBLISHER	GRADE RANGE	CATEGORY	TOPIC(S)	LOCATION
USA ATLAS 5.0	CD-ROM	Mindscape	4 and up	Reference	Geography	Library
WORLD ATLAS 5.0	CD-ROM	Mindscape	4 and up	Reference	Geography	Library
1995 MULTIMEDIA ENCYCLOPEDIA	CD-ROM	Groliers	4 and up	Reference		Library
THINKING THINGS I	CD-ROM	Edmark	PreK–2	Skill Building	Critical Thinking	LS-2RB
THINKING THINGS I	CD-ROM	Edmark	PreK–2	Skill Building	Critical Thinking	LS-1M, Library
THE SAN DIEGO ZOO PRESENTS: THE ANIMALS 2.0	CD-ROM	Mindscape	2 and up	Reference	Science	LS-1M
GREAT WONDERS OF THE WORLD	CD-ROM			Reference	Geography	LS-2L
THE SAN DIEGO ZOO PRESENTS: THE ANIMALS 2.0	CD-ROM	Mindscape	2 and up	Reference	Science	LS-2RB
JUST GRANDMA AND ME	CD-ROM	Broderbund	PreK–4	Skill Building	Language Arts	LS-K
THE SAN DIEGO ZOO PRESENTS: THE ANIMALS 2.0	CD-ROM	Mindscape	2 and up	Reference	Science	LS-Science Lab
THE WAY THINGS WORK	CD-ROM	Dorling Kindersley	2 and up	Discovery	Science	LS-Science Lab
1995 MULTIMEDIA ENCYCLOPEDIA	CD-ROM	Groliers	4 and up	Reference		MS-4J
USA ATLAS 5.0	CD-ROM	Mindscape	4 and up	Reference	Geography	MS-4T
WORLD ATLAS 5.0	CD-ROM	Mindscape	4 and up	Reference	Geography	MS-4T
MULTIMEDIA ENCYCLOPEDIA	CD-ROM	Compton's	4 and up	Reference		MS-4T
USA ATLAS 5.0	CD-ROM	Mindscape	4 and up	Reference	Geography	MS-5F
WORLD ATLAS 5.0	CD-ROM	Mindscape	4 and up	Reference	Geography	MS-5F
1995 MULTIMEDIA ENCYCLOPEDIA	CD-ROM	Groliers	4 and up	Reference		MS-5F
USA ATLAS 2.0	CD-ROM	Mindscape	4 and up	Reference	Geography	MS-5M
WORLD ATLAS 3.0	CD-ROM	Mindscape	4 and up	Reference	Geography	MS-5M

MAP M, continued

SOFTWARE PURCHASES '95—SORTED

CD-ROM TITLE	TYPE	PUBLISHER	GRADE RANGE	CATEGORY	TOPIC(S)	LOCATION
1994 MULTIMEDIA ENCYCLOPEDIA	CD-ROM	Groliers	4 and up	Reference		MS-5M
WEBSTER'S 9TH NEW COLLEGIATE DICTIONARY	CD-ROM			Reference		MS-5M
USA ATLAS 5.0	CD-ROM	Mindscape	4 and up	Reference	Geography	MS-6H, Library
WORLD ATLAS 5.0	CD-ROM	Mindscape	4 and up	Reference	Geography	MS-6H, Library
1995 MULTIMEDIA ENCYCLOPEDIA	CD-ROM	Groliers	4 and up	Reference		MS-6H, Library
1992 MULTIMEDIA ENCYCLOPEDIA	CD-ROM	Groliers	4 and up	Reference		MS-6KR
THINKING THINGS II	3.5 diskette	Edmark	K-6	Skill Building	Critical Thinking	MS-4J
THINKING THINGS II	3.5 diskette	Edmark	K-6	Skill Building	Critical Thinking	MS-4T
A.D.A.M.: THE INSIDE STORY					Science	US-Science
THE SAN DIEGO ZOO PRESENTS: THE ANIMALS 2.0	CD-ROM	Mindscape	2 and up	Reference	Science	US-Science Lab
INSECTS: A WORLD OF DISCOVERY	CD-ROM	CSIRO	4 and up	Reference	Science	US-Science Lab
AMERICA ONLINE	3.5 diskette					

MAP N

2ND GRADE CURRICULUM MAP

	CONTENT	SKILLS	ASSESSMENTS
SEPTEMBER	Def. of a noun, proper noun, verb, adj.	Identify noun as person, place, thing Compare a proper noun with common noun Identify a verb as an action word Recognize verbs Identify adj. as describing word Recognize adj.	The Big Four Make a book showing common nouns and proper nouns, adj.. verbs Demonstrate verbs through charades
	Alphabetize to 1st, 2nd letter Review short & long vowel sounds	Understand order of the alphabet Recognize letter placement Identify different vowel sounds	Write words to 1st and 2nd letter Put spelling words in ABC order Test
OCTOBER	Define antonyms, synonyms, homonyms, Learn that each word has syllables Teach tongue twisters as alliteration Teach compound words Teach the 5 parts of a Friendly letter Teach a simile as comparison using like or as	Identify an antonym, synonym, homonym Apply them in your writing Identify syllables in a word Compare syllables in different words Understand that each syllable has vowel sound Discriminate sounds as being the same Identify and form compound words Identify the 5 parts of friendly letter Understand the 5 parts and where they go Identify and form similes, apply in writing	The Big Four "nym" step books Clap it out Toss the bean bag at each each syllable Musical instruments Write alliteration sentences using their names Cut compound words from magazines Label a letter with the 5 parts Write a letter to a friend Write your own similes in a poem
NOVEMBER	Teach plural as meaning more than 1 Singular means 1 Rules for spelling plurals Irregular plurals Public Speaking	Identify plurals and singulars Form plurals and singulars using s, es, ies (rules) Identify regular and irregular plurals Memorizing and familiarizing themselves with rhyming words related to the Thanksgiving theme	Make a plural counting book The Big Four Plural handouts Recitation of lines in Thanksgiving Presentation
DECEMBER	Fiction vs. Nonfiction Poetry Dictionary Skills Main Idea	Identify literature as fiction or nonfiction Identify similes and couplets Identify Haiku and Cinquain Identify guide and entry words Identify definition according to content Identify topic of story main idea and details	Create a nonfiction book Write and decorate seasonal poems Look up spelling words for the week and tell what page it is on, what the guide words are, tell what the definition is Answer related comprehension questions and orally retell story

MAP O

4TH GRADE CURRICULUM MAP

TIME FRAME	CONTENT	SKILLS	ASSESSMENT
SEPTEMBER/OCTOBER ½ NOVEMBER	Reading: Sarah, Plain and Tall 1) What are the characteristics of a historical fiction? 2) What are the parts of a character analysis? 3) What is a literature discussion? 4) What are parts of a story?	-using evidence from a story to answer questions -parts of a story: setting, characters, plot -elements of character analysis Physical description Personality traits Why is the character important to the story?	-literature discussions -comprehension checks Response journal -character analysis
	Grammar/Spelling: 200 most troublesome words	-nouns-common & proper -adjectives -singular/plural -sub./verb agreement	Mug shot quizzes (editing) -bimonthly tests -dictation
	Composition: Describe Mode Poetry	-opening and closing -supporting details -paragraphing sense -writing process (introduce all steps, focus on brainstorming)	-revision of writing sample -character analysis -poem
	● Poetry - Jack Prelutsky	-public speaking skills	poetry recitations
½ NOVEMBER DECEMBER/JANUARY	Reading: Kneeknock Rise 1) What are the characteristics of a fable? 2) What is the problem and resolution of a story? 3) What are main events and supporting details of a story?	-rising and falling action -climax -conflict and resolution -main events -context clues to determine meaning	-literature discussions -comprehension checks -tests -write a summary of main events -character analysis
	Grammar/Spelling: 200 Most troublesome words Content Words	-subject/predicate -pronouns and antecedent -adverbs -possession – singular and plural -commas	-bimonthly spelling tests -mug shot quizzes (editing) -dictation
	Composition: Narrative Mode	-catchy opening sentence -using 5 senses to describe -varied sentence beginnings -narrowing topic – writing process (focus on revision and editing)	-short story in narrative mode
JANUARY	Composition (con't.): Imaginative Mode (Poetry) Hailstones and Halibut Bones	-imagery -figurative language similes/metaphors -analysis of Prelutsky's style	-color poems
	● Poetry - Prelutsky	- public speaking skills -point of view	-poem modeled after Prelutsky's style -recitation of poem with actions
	Reading: The Sign of the Beaver	-main idea and supporting details	

MAP O, continued

4TH GRADE CURRICULUM MAP

TIME FRAME	CONTENT	SKILLS	ASSESSMENT
FEBRUARY/MARCH APRIL	1) How do you write from a different point of view? 2) How do you write a book review? 3) What is theme? 4) What are the characteristics of a realistic fiction/historical fiction? 5) How do you write a news story? Grammar/Spelling: 200 Most Troublesome Words Content words Composition: Imaginative Mode • Poetry Exposition Mode How To	-parts of a book review Description of setting, characters, plot, author's theme -topic sentence -5 W's -root words -prefixes and suffixes -using dictionary to define prefixes and suffixes -quotation marks -context clues to determine correct meaning in dictionary -writing process (focus on revision and editing) -personification -quotation marks -sequencing -sentence length -vocabulary words (better words for said, walk, etc.)–using a thesaurus -free verse -precise words -transition words -paragraphing sense	-journal from a character's point of view -book review -news show including feature story, weather, sports, commercial -bimonthly spelling tests -dictation -Mug Shot quizzes (editing) -short story in imaginative mode -poem and recitation - how to -book review (be the character) -character analysis (verbally) -literature discussions -culminating activity
APRIL/MAY	• Poetry – Myra Cohn Livingston Reading: Black Beauty, Dear Mr. Henshaw, Twenty-One Balloons 1) What is the author's purpose? 2) What genre does each book fall into and why?	-sequencing -public speaking -parts of a story -criticism of text -literature discussions -author's purpose -logical prediction -responding to text -commas	
MAY/JUNE	Grammar/Spelling: 200 Most Troublesome Words Content Words		-bimonthly tests -Mug Shot quizzes (editing) -dictation
MAY/JUNE	Composition: Persuasive Mode Poetry	-audience sense -paragraphing -strong conclusion -topic sentence with supporting details -writing process -fact vs. opinion	-persuasive essay

MAP P

CURRICULUM MAP FOR M.S. SEMINAR SERIES

	CONTENT	SKILLS	ASSESSMENT
SEPTEMBER	Environmental and Community: A. - Valuing Scientific Literacy - definitions and environmental impact (8-week project) B. - Media, Campaign, Public Opinion (Project will last till November elections)	-A. Define and relate science and environment; analyze two sources in news media (newspapers, magazines, Internet); identify scientific concepts and explain their importance to scientific literacy; access local, national congressional records and identify laws that deal with science issues; analyze law and identify the science concepts needed to understand the laws. -B. Media - analyze news comparing/contrasting sources used (print, TV, Internet); analyze and identify slogans; debunk/decode news	-A. Concept map - rubric, summary science news; critical essay (environmental laws) -B. Journal of recorded slogans citing dates, targeted audience, biased words - due week of election - weekly submission of 2 news stories from 3 sources
OCTOBER	Environment and Community - see September for (A) and (B). - Morality, ethics, dilemma.	- Create moral dilemma, including the 5 essential components using the environment + political campaign of 1996; - present original dilemma to a large group; lead group discussion on original dilemma.	- See September for (A) and (B). - Written moral dilemma; class rubrics. Class presentation of dilemma including student led discussion evaluated by teacher/students generated rubric.
NOVEMBER	Community/Balance - See (A) and (B) September - Murder, Mischief and Mayhem (M, M, & M). - Science Literacy - Simulated Town Meeting.	- M, M & M - research original sources (NY Times Index, Reader's Guide, Book Review Digest) write creative research paper on an unsolved crime; - research, organize and conduct simulated town meeting; - identify process decision making concerning environmental policies	- creative research paper; simulated town meeting - class rubric
DECEMBER	Community/Family: Gift of Quotes. - Environment/Balance: Science Project	- Utilize reference books (Bartlet's Bk. Of Quotes, etc.); select appropriate quotes and artistic vehicle; create literary/artistic gift of quotes; - research, journalize, report, using IMRAD form, the results of science project	- Gift of Quotes. - Science Project - journal, report.
JANUARY	World Communities: Museum Unit (to run through February) - Role of museums in preserving societal values, selected societies, cultures, time periods.	- Study history of museum exhibits, museum organization, and the role of staff in creating them.	- Museum display showcasing selected society, culture, time period.

MAP P, continued

CURRICULUM MAP FOR M.S. SEMINAR SERIES

	CONTENT	SKILLS	ASSESSMENT
FEBRUARY	Balance/World Communities: Museum Unit - see January Museum Unit (see content, skills and assessment) Tesselations.	- Use geometric constructions to create tessellations. - Show the relevance between tessellations and world culture.	Student generated tessellations.
MARCH	Balance/World Communities: See February re tessellations (content, skills, and assessment). Poetry - famous multicultural poems.	- Analyze poetry from different cultures. - Identify values/figurative languages/literary techniques popular worldwide.	Position paper on role of tessellations in religious expression of cultures. Poem translation and analysis. Original peoms.
APRIL	Future: - Beginning of the end: Sci. Fict. Story going from last line back to tell a story. - Scientific concepts in science fiction.	- To go from a conclusion back to the starting point. - Analyze science fiction short story. - Identify predominant sci. Concepts used by author. - Explain science behind concept.	- Student generated short story. - Build a model depicting a sci. Concept as identified in the short story.
MAY	Future/World Communities. - D-Day survival scenario for end of world. - The flight of the Maple Copter.	- To problem solve in groups. - To create survival strategy based on given constrains (scientific and societal). - To present and defend strategy to large group. - Lead group discussion. - Apply sci. Method to natural phenomena. - Design an original experiment. - Build a model. - Write research paper using IMRAD	- Oral presentation using students generated rubric. - Survival strategy. - Model of flying maple copter. - Science fiction story.
JUNE	See May, Yearly Projects	- Oral presentation in which students present their successes and failures.	- Yearly Project.

MAP Q

HIGH SCHOOL PHYSICS CURRICULUM MAP

	CONTENT	SKILLS	ASSESSMENT
SEPTEMBER	Measuring systems Uncertainties in measurement Vector addition	Make measurements in SI units Present the results of an experiment as a lab report Use a computer graphing program Add vectors using trigonometry Use significant figures in collecting and manipulating data Analyze graphs of data for slope and the equation of the line	Written lab reports Tests: problems, multiple choice, essay Lab performance
OCTOBER	Linear motion Vector addition Acceleration of gravity	Vector addition continued Analyze the effect of forces on motion Use algebra to solve equations for motion Represent the motion of a body as position vs. Time and velocity vs. Time graphs from lab data Determine the acceleration of gravity in the lab	Written lab reports Tests: problems, multiple choice, essay Lab performance Scientist report (library research) Oral presentation of group problem-solving activity
NOVEMBER	Newton's Laws of Motion Forces Torque	Add force vectors using trigonometry as well as in the lab Draw free body diagrams to isolate the forces acting on a body For a body in equilibrium, show that EA. = 0 and write equations to represent this Analyze force problems involving friction, inclines, and torques.	Written lab reports Tests: problems, multiple choice, essay Lab performance Lab report written in the IMRAD form
DECEMBER	Motion in two dimensions Centripetal forces Gravitation	ID Real and fictitious forces Use algebra to solve sets of equations relating the vertical and horizontal components of 2D motion Describe gravitation as one of the forces of nature	Written lab reports Tests: problems, multiple choice, essay Lab performance Design problem "10m vehicle"

MAP Q, continued

HIGH SCHOOL PHYSICS CURRICULUM MAP

	CONTENT	SKILLS	ASSESSMENT
JANUARY	Work Energy, potential & kinetic Momentum	To relate work, energy, and power Write equations representing the law of conservation on momentum for systems	Written lab reports Tests: problems, multiple choice, essay Lab performance Midterm Exam
FEBRUARY	Kinetic Theory Heat	Write equations to describe the exchange of heat in a system including any phase changes which may occur. Relate the structure of matter to the properties of the different phases of matter	Written lab reports Tests: problems, multiple choice, essay Lab performance
MARCH	Waves Sound Light	Predict the results of wave interactions Analyze a system with moving source or observer to predict the change in frequency of an emitted sound using Doppler effect concepts Relate the properties of light to its dual nature	Written lab reports Tests: problems, multiple choice, essay Lab performance Design project
APRIL	Electrostatics Current Electricity	Use the laws of electrostatics to predict the results of induction and conduction effects on charged bodies Interpret and analyze field diagrams	Written lab reports Tests: problems, multiple choice, essay Lab performance IMRAD lab report Field diagram analysis
MAY	DC circuits Magnetism Nuclear Physics	Use Ohm's and Kirchoff's laws to analyze solve circuit diagrams Set up circuits in the laboratory Evaluate the benefits vs. the risks of nuclear energy and radioisotope use in terms of the properties of radiation	Written lab reports Tests: problems, multiple choice, essay Lab performance Position paper RE nuclear energy Circuit diagram analysis
JUNE	Astronomy	Complete the assignments and projects in the Astronomy packet and prepare a portfolio of these activities	Compile portfolio of astronomy assignments FINAL EXAM